PLEASE HUG ME

I'VE BEEN DELAYED

PLEASE HUG ME

I'VE BEEN DELAYED

THE **ONLY GUIDE YOU'LL EVER NEED** TO
SURVIVE THE **NOT-SO-FRIENDLY SKIES**

JEFF MICHAELS

GREENLEAF
BOOK GROUP PRESS

Published by Greenleaf Book Group Press
Austin, TX
www.greenleafbookgroup.com

Design and composition by Greenleaf Book Group LLC
Cover design by Greenleaf Book Group LLC

Publisher's Cataloging-In-Publication Data
(Prepared by The Donohue Group, Inc.)

Michaels, Jeff.
  Please hug me—I've been delayed : the only guide you'll ever need to survive the not-so-friendly skies / Jeff Michaels. -- 1st ed.

  p. : ill. ; cm.

  Includes index.
  ISBN: 978-1-60832-020-2

1. Air travel--Humor. 2. Air travel--Handbooks, manuals, etc. 3. American wit and humor. I. Title.

HE9787 .M53 2010
387.742   2009932099

Part of the Tree Neutral™ program, which offsets the number of trees consumed in the production and printing of this book by taking proactive steps, such as planting trees in direct proportion to the number of trees used: www.treeneutral.com

TreeNeutral

Printed in the United States of America on acid-free paper

09 10 11 12 13 14   10 9 8 7 6 5 4 3 2 1

First Edition

This book is dedicated to my parents—such wonderful people,
I'd sit through any delay just to visit.

CONTENTS

PREBOARDING ANNOUNCEMENT

Hello Fellow Traveler!

If you've picked up this book, chances are you are one of the nearly eight hundred million passengers who take to what I like to refer to as the "not-so-friendly skies" each year in the United States. Quite possibly you are doing your best deep-breathing exercises to avoid slamming your head through a sheet of glass as disaster has struck yet again. A disaster so horrid you can't even speak its name. A disaster so gruesome, the mere thought of it sends shivers down your spine and brings you to your knees.

No, I'm not talking about the Spice Girls, Golden Years reunion tour. I'm talking about those five terrifying words: *Your flight has been delayed.* There is no greater threat to your sanity in the universe.

Yes friend, those words mean disaster has struck. Doomsday has arrived. You are facing the horror of hours upon hours of hideous boredom in an airport where you've already spent so much time that you are regularly receiving your mail there. Or perhaps you are sitting through an interminably long flight, praying you graze a snowcapped peak and the oxygen masks fall from the ceiling because the passenger next to you has thoughtlessly eaten nothing but beans for three days straight. Or perhaps you're one of the thousands of stranded passengers left shivering in the cold after ditching all your clothes on the side of the road, unable to come up with the $50 luggage fee. Do you really need more than a T-shirt and one pair of underwear for a two-week vacation? (The airlines don't believe so.)

Or maybe you're a parent and the proud head of a family of five, stuck having to choose which kid you're going to leave at the ticket counter, because as it turns out, there are only four open seats on the next available flight. Well, little Jim was the mistake anyway . . .

Or perhaps you've just had your favorite tube of toothpaste confiscated by security. The one with the minty-tasting green specs that make your breath feel so amazingly fresh that you just can't bear to leave home without it. (Unless this is your first flight, you should realize that more than 3 ounces of toothpaste is a threat to national security.) But we're not here to reprimand. We're here to educate. So don't be so hard on yourself. You are not alone in this sea of weary airline passengers . . . though you may be the one with the smelliest breath. Maybe you should grab a pack of gum while contemplating your next move.

Remember the days when you booked an airline ticket, and there was actually a chance your flight wouldn't be overbooked, your plane would be on time, *and* your luggage would arrive at an airport fairly close to the one you landed in? Those were crazy times, weren't they?

Remember when you didn't have to take off every stitch of clothing just to convince the security agents that your private parts are not, nor have they ever been, made of metal? Or when you didn't have to frantically consult the advanced calculus function on your BlackBerry to determine how many ounces of shampoo and conditioner (and minty-green toothpaste) you were allowed to bring on board?

Remember when you could carry your own reasonably priced bottle of water on to a plane, instead of having to pay $5 for a TSA-approved bottle of Homeland Security Super Water? Remember when you used to get excited about getting aboard a big ol' jet airliner, and flying to new and exotic destinations? Taking the family on a much-needed vacation instead of plopping them in a twelve-foot kiddie pool in the backyard and paying an unemployed computer worker to come dress up like Mickey Mouse and convince them they're at Disney World?[1]

Can't remember those days? Me neither.

Welcome to the new world of air travel.

Oh, but it's not all bad. We still have one of the most sophisticated air fleets in the world, taking off and touching down in sleek new airports filled with snazzy modern art, futuristic moving sidewalks, and flat-screen television monitors (so you can see in crystal-sharp, high-definition detail precisely how long you are going to be stuck in this sleek new airport).

We've got satellite TV in virtually every seatback, movies and video games on demand, and the ability to text message other passengers on the same flight (so you can discreetly ask the passenger next to you to stop passing gas). And we even have an 80 percent chance of arriving at the same destination as our luggage. That's pretty good. That's almost 81 percent.

Yet, even with all this technology, something is missing from air travel. I take that back. Everything is missing from air travel. But I'm here to tell you it doesn't have to be this way. While many things like bad weather and the soaring price of jet fuel are certainly beyond our control, with a little knowledge, we can at least make our journeys a lot more entertaining.

---

1. Unemployed computer workers make the best Disney character impersonators because they're used to not talking all day at work, and are rarely over six-feet tall, so they fit the costumes well.

Take a look outside the window (if your particular airline doesn't charge to raise the shades). See the pretty sun? See the majestic white clouds lazily floating by? The skies are the same as they've always been—it's the game that's changed. You just need to learn how to play it. So sit back, put your tray tables in the upright position, and let's see what we can do to help make your skies friendly once again.

Hopefully you'll never again have to hear the dreaded words, "Your flight has been delayed." But if you do, at least you'll have a new friend to keep you company—me. Providing you buy this book of course. You should—I worked hard on it, because I've been where you are far more times than I care to recall, and I've learned a thing or two along the way. And it is my sincere wish to share this knowledge with you.

Oh, and by the way, just in case you end up having to spend the entire evening in the terminal, the specially designed soft cover serves as a fairly comfy pillow. Also, in Appendix 1 you'll find a little something to help get you through the night. The first of my many gifts to you.

So let's get settled in and begin where all flights originate: on the ground.

My sincerest wishes for your safe and happy travels, and everlasting freedom from bean eaters, bungled baggage, and bellowing babies.

CHAPTER 1

ON THE GROUND

$1,700 for a ticket to Detroit? Are you f#%@ing kidding me?

A Brief History of Flight

- 5000 BC: Man witnesses bird in flight and dreams of one day soaring through the majestic skies.
- February 1, 1900 AD: Woman gets fed up and tells her husband she won't give him any more sex unless he takes her on a proper vacation.
- February 2, 1900 AD: Man invents the airplane.

The very first flight occurred on December 17, 1903, in Kitty Hawk, North Carolina, and lasted exactly twelve seconds. Barely time to get the drinks served and the movie started before it was time to put the tray tables up and prepare for landing.

Since then, air travel has expanded to a multigazillion-dollar industry, with airlines operating in virtually every country in the world, and hundreds of thousands of planes and airline workers carrying nearly two billion passengers around the globe each year. Proving once again that mankind can achieve the impossible, then go right back to lounging on the couch for another century.

While the invention of the airplane was no doubt incredible for its time, we've sort of slacked on making any improvements recently. We still need giant runways to get these massive beasts off the ground. We still haven't secured the rights from Paramount to use the warp engines from *Star Trek* to get us some real speed. And we still can't manage to build a plane that averages more than a half mile to the gallon. Instead of solving problems, we just make more kids. Kids are smart these days. They can beat video games. They'll figure something out.

But before your honor student is old enough to solve the global transportation crisis, you're gonna have to take her to Disney World so she doesn't write a report on "Why My Summer Vacation Sucked." And you're gonna have to fly.

And if you think $1,700 is a lot for a ticket to Detroit, just wait until they announce they messed up a few dozen zeroes when they

Do You Care?

First Flight Fun Facts

Wilbur Wright beat out his younger brother, Orville, to become the very first pilot in history by the toss of a coin. Lucky bastard.

Including Orville, only six people witnessed the first human flight. Hundreds were invited, but it was cold out. And Oprah was running a best-of special that morning.

The Wright brothers actually made four successful flights that infamous day before their flying machine was wrecked by a giant gust of wind, immediately putting their startup airline out of business. Not to be outdone, in 2001 the Canadian airline Roots Air gave the brothers a run for their money, collapsing after just forty-one days in operation. Oh Canada, you try so very hard. You've earned your A for effort.

were estimating how much oil is left in the ground, and we've only got a year's supply left. That'll be fun.

In the meantime, let's start off with some tips to keep as much money in your pocket as you possibly can!

TIPS FOR NEGOTIATING THE LOWEST TICKET PRICE IMAGINABLE. LIKE $1.86 ROUND-TRIP (PLUS TAX).

Thankfully, Al Gore invented the Internet so we no longer have to stay on hold for hours at a time when trying to purchase an airline ticket. But now, everywhere you click it seems some company you've never heard of is promising you the absolute lowest fare to whatever city you want to visit.[2] Orbitz, Expedia, Travelocity, Hotwire, Cheapfares, Priceline, *The Price Is Right*, Tony Danza's Bargain Basement Travel Deals . . . where do you start???

Wouldn't it be great if there were *one* place you could go to get every fare from every airline all at once? If there were a website that tied everything together into one tidy listing of flights with all the major carriers and easy-to-use sorting features?

Um, there is: Sidestep.com.

Simply log on, enter your travel dates and destination, and let Sidestep do its thing. After you find the flight and fare that's right for you, Sidestep will generally take you to the airline's website to complete the purchase. It's always a good idea to book your ticket directly through an airline if you can. In the event your flight is cancelled or, dare I speak

---

2. Ever wonder how those little ads on the right of your screen all pop up with low-fare offers to the exact city you want to visit, seemingly by coincidence? It's no accident. Google spends billions of dollars each year installing hidden microphones in every home in America to monitor conversations and find out what consumers are considering purchasing, then creating personalized marketing campaigns based on this information. (Just kidding. The microphones are in your iPhone.)

the word, delayed, the airlines will do a much better job notifying you of any changes.[3] In fact, some airlines will automatically reroute you should they determine a delay will cause you to miss your connecting flight, long before you even get to the airport.

And remember, it's a big country. Just because it's sunny outside your little kitchen window doesn't mean there isn't golf ball–size hail tearing through the skies of Chicago, Atlanta, Denver, or any other major city in a region with a violent, unpredictable weather pattern, thus considered by the FAA to be an excellent location for a major airline hub. (Why not just route all connecting flights through the Bermuda Triangle and be done with it?) Unpredictable weather is just one of the many reasons why you should *always* call and check your flight status before you venture out to fight traffic for the three-hour commute to the airport.

You do always call . . . right?

Returning to Sidestep, they've got plenty of advanced options too, like selecting nonstop flights only, or checking "no turbo props," for those of you worried about flying in a plane not much bigger than a bus. And if you're feeling lonely, you can sign up for the Sidestep newsletter and receive weekly updates and handy travel discounts.

There is even a special buzz section for travel ideas, targeted for those with lots of money and no imagination: "Top Nude Beaches," "Top 10 Outrageous Bathrooms," or "Top Destinations for a Babymoon," the latest trend for expecting parents. Every destination guaranteed to be warm, sunny, and remind you of the life you'll no longer

---

3. Unless you enjoy showing up at the airport to fly home for Christmas and being informed the earliest flight they can get you on is sometime in June because the discount ticket site (which shall be nameless but starts with O and rhymes with Lenny Kravitz) you booked your ticket through did a piss-poor job of informing you that your flight was cancelled weeks ago, resulting in missing Christmas Eve with your family and the next several months spent writing a bitter air-travel guide. If you're one of those revenge-seeking humor-writer types who enjoys that type of thing, then definitely go for it.

have after you deliver your global-transportation-problem-solving kid into the world.

And nope, no endorsement deal here. I simply enjoy pointing out a good product when I see it. Although I fully encourage Sidestep.com to contact me via the publisher to send some free goodies. (I'm a size medium T-shirt.)

Customer Testimonials

Wow. I used to spend hours searching for flights online. Now it only takes a few minutes. Sidestep is amazing. How come I haven't heard of it before?

—Jim, Seattle, Washington

Hi Jim. Dunno. It's been around since 2000. You should probably get out more.

Dear Jeff. Thanks a lot. (Sarcastic.) My mother-in-law read your stupid book and now she visits us once a month because it's "so easy" for her to book her ticket. You suck.

—Brad, Baltimore, Maryland

Oh, uh, sorry about that Brad. Your mother-in-law sounds sweet. See chapter 2 on how to put her on the No-Fly list.

This all sounds wonderful. But what if I don't own a computer or have access to this Internet?

—Nancy, Detroit, Michigan

Hi Nancy. Are you friends with Jim in Seattle by any chance . . . ?

CONAN O'BRIEN: THE LATE SHOW LOW-FARE LOWDOWN

Most people know that the least expensive days to fly are Tuesdays and Wednesdays. (And if you didn't, now you do!) It stands to reason that since a large majority of travel occurs on weekends, you can find much lower fares traveling during the week. Not to mention the obvious benefits of shorter security lines, less-stressed airline employees, and better in-flight TV choices.

But do you know the *one* time of the week when you should book your ticket to guarantee you're paying the lowest price offered? Read on.

Without getting into a boring lesson on macroeconomics (I couldn't stay awake through it in college—I'm certainly not going to include it here), it does help to know that airlines basically work like your neighborhood gas stations. The major carriers like to raise their prices late in the day on Fridays (greedy bastards), because they know people tend to book their tickets when they are home on the weekends, planning their vacations to Disney World with their screaming kids. Unfortunately for you, this is the *worst* time to buy a ticket.

By Saturday morning the major competitors will generally jump in and match any fare increases. Over the weekend the airlines will be jockeying to see exactly what the market will bear. Prices can rise quickly and dramatically. Alternatively, if other airlines fail to match the original increase, the fare may drop back down on Sunday night or early Monday morning.

Now, if you hopped online on Saturday and booked your ticket at the higher fare, pardon my French, but you're screwed. You may be able to exchange your ticket for the lower fare, but you're gonna get stuck with a $100 or more change fee—per ticket.

So Sunday night then? I should stay up late and call in sick for work on Monday?

No, late Sunday nights are not always the answer. Depending on how the weekend goes, the airlines may carry the fare into the week. But what's the one thing smaller airlines can use to lure customers away from their loyalty to the major airlines? Offer an even cheaper fare. (We would've also accepted free drink coupons, or more peanuts.) By Monday or Tuesday, all of the major airlines may scramble to match this lower fare.

Okay. Tuesday, and I'm golden, right?

Easy cowboy. You're involved in a full-scale war at this point, and wars can be highly unpredictable. There is some debate as to whether Tuesday or Wednesday is the actual best day to book your ticket. Some claim that around midnight on Wednesday the airlines purge all the low-cost fares people put on hold on Tuesday that were not purchased within twenty-four hours, leaving some juicy fares prime for the picking.

Some folks say this is a myth. Mere folklore. As ridiculous as believing in Bigfoot, the Loch Ness Monster, or that the LA Clippers will ever win the NBA Championship. Maybe. Truth is, airline pricing is an industry secret kept under tighter security than who truly killed JFK or the recipe for Coca-Cola. Even the people who set the prices don't know what they're going to do next. It's like the world's biggest game of Texas Hold 'Em. But keep in mind that Wednesday is hump day. And when people hump, they mellow out. Taking the consumer for every dollar they have no longer seems important. So go ahead. Call their bluff. And then I can buy my ticket on Tuesday.

All right. So what's any of this got to do with Conan O'Brien? And why does he lick his fingers and wipe his eyebrows so much? Leno never did that.

It's simple. The Conan show is not on during the weekends, and a lot of Mondays he gets lazy and takes the night off. And everyone knows that on Thursdays and Fridays he's got the B-list actors and subpar musical guests. If you can't remember what day and time to book your ticket, just wait until the good Conan shows come on, which is Tuesday and Wednesday nights right before midnight, and that is when you should book your ticket.[4]

Conan will keep you company into the wee hours of the morning with his witty monologue, zippy one-liners, and his little trick when he pretends he's a puppet and then snips the imaginary strings on his legs and nearly falls over. And don't forget to consider the time zone in which your airline is headquartered. (See chart.) You may end up staying up far later than you hoped—but the savings could be well worth it.

How about that $2 fare you were bragging about? Where's that Mr. Airfare Genius?

I'm getting to it. But I've got a short story I think everyone might enjoy first . . .

I vividly recall my high school teacher Mr. McNeal bragging about how he found a misprinted newspaper ad offering airline tickets for $40 and was taking his entire family to Florida for spring vacation. We all ran home and tried to get our parents to call in and get the same deal, dreaming of a week filled with lightning-fast roller coasters and endless Disney magic, but of course, the airline had already printed a correction. (Well, I actually walked home. I knew my dad would've said, "We'll, now, let's not go crazy here. Let's wait and see if it drops to $20." My sister and I weren't getting mouse ears anytime soon.)

But that can't happen anymore now that we've got the Internet, right? Don't be so sure. In April 2005, due to a computer glitch (or a

---

4. Please note: Do not call Conan O'Brien if you don't end up with an airfare to your liking. He's only one man. And if you prefer another late-night TV show host to serve as your mnemonic device, by all means use him.

Airline Corporate Headquarters by Time Zone

Eastern Standard Time (EST)
- Air Force One: Washington, DC
- AirTran Airways: Orlando, Florida
- Delta Air Lines: Atlanta, Georgia
- JetBlue Airways: Forest Hills, New York
- Sandpiper Airlines (the little airline from *Wings*): Nantucket, Massachusetts

Central Standard Time (CST)
- American Airlines: Fort Worth, Texas
- United Airlines: Chicago, Illinois
- Midwest Airlines: Oak Creek, Wisconsin
- Continental Airlines: Houston, Texas
- Southwest Airlines: Dallas, Texas

Mountain Time Zone (MNT)
- Frontier Airlines: Denver, Colorado
- US Airways: Tempe, Arizona

Pacific Time Zone (PST)
- Alaska Airlines: Seattle, Washington
- Virgin America: Burlingame, California

Hawaiian Time Zone (HST)
- Hawaiian Airlines: Honolulu, Hawaii

lazy intern), US Airways ended up selling tickets for several hours for $1.86 (plus tax) to cities nationwide. If you're determined to fly for the absolute lowest price possible, it may just be worth your while to quit your day job and monitor the Internet 24/7 for the next two-dollar deal to come along.

Or better yet, put your kids to work. Let them scan for deals while you take a nap.

PREDICTING THE FUTURE, ONE AIRFARE AT A TIME

Once you finally find the airfare you want, do you break into a cold sweat when you reach the Confirm Purchase page, because you *know* as soon as you click the button the price will go down? Do you get up repeatedly each night until the day of your flight to see if your ticket price dropped? Do you poll everyone on your flight to see how much they paid for their tickets? Do you still use your checkbook at the grocery store?

Okay, the grocery store one I can't help you with. You've got to learn to let go. But if you suffer from the debilitating fear that you missed the *absolute lowest price* for your airfare, you are not alone. Short of camping out in front of the computer for months at a time, you can never know for certain. If you want to try to avoid all this silliness, pay a visit to the travel page at Bing.com.

Using Farecast technology, Bing.com will actually predict whether or not your particular fare is likely to go up or down in the near future, based on the past several years of historical pricing data. The little green, orange, and red arrows indicate if you should buy now or hold off on your purchase, much like a stock program analyzes past performance of a stock and spits out its recommendation. They are basically like a virtual friend standing over your shoulder, encouraging you to go ahead, click that button. Things will be okay. (And you thought the Internet was only good for porn.)

Booking Tip: Take Care of Numero Uno

If you are searching for tickets for your entire family, try enter-
ing just one passenger at a time and see if you get a cheaper
price. If an airline only has one ticket remaining at a certain
fare class and you request two or more, they will automatically
bump you to the next price level. By searching for one ticket at
a time, you may be able to book one at the cheaper fare. Then,
simply go back and book the other tickets and select seats next
to each other. Or, you may choose to sit separately. Might be a
nice break from your unappreciative kids, or a chance to meet
someone new and spice up your marriage.

Again, I'm just reporting the goods here. Not getting any kick-
backs. But, ahem, size medium T-shirts fit me nicely. Dark colors pre-
ferred. (Within a year of writing this book, I sincerely hope to amass a
complete new wardrobe of travel company logo shirts.)

Some other discount sites are starting to offer similar price guar-
antees too, like that one that starts with *O* and rhymes with Lenny
Kravits. So feel free to shop around. But I'm still not recommending
them until I get my apology letter for forgetting to tell me my flight
was cancelled and making me miss Christmas Eve dinner.

SPIRITUAL ENLIGHTENMENT FOR YOUR BOTTOM

Have you ever burst into tears immediately after takeoff when you
tried to push the little button on your armrest and then noticed the

sticker on the window and realized you somehow managed to find the *one* seat on the plane that doesn't recline, due to Federal Regulation 121.310(f)(3)? (Or am I the only overemotional flyer?) Or have you found yourself wishing for death to come claim you after spending an entire flight seated next to a leaky lavatory? With a little preparation, you can avoid catastrophes like this in the future.

The good news is virtually every major airline now allows you to choose your own seat when booking your flight online. The bad news is, virtually every major airline now allows you to choose your own seat when booking your flight online.

For many, this added decision in the already stressful booking process is one more unwanted headache. No longer does it suffice to say you prefer a window or an aisle, and let the airline gods randomly assign you. You've got to do it yourself, which brings about a whole new level of anxiety. What if I get stuck next to a crying baby? What if I pick a seat next to someone with the bird flu? What if I screw myself and book a seat in the peanut-free buffer zone and get stuck with pretzels? (See chapter 6, "What Happened to the Peanuts?") Which kid should I put closer to the exit row, the smart one who can help others, or the one we're not too worried about losing?

Relax. Take a hit off your asthma inhaler and read on. In essence, when you are booking your own seat, you are deciding your own destiny. The problem is, people don't like choosing their own destiny. They much prefer to be told what to do.[5] Thankfully, there's a solution.

---

5. If you don't believe this to be true, a recent survey revealed that the number one cause for anxiety on airplanes is not turbulence, a sudden loss of cabin pressure, or even being hijacked. It's what to choose for a snack. Most domestic flights have more than a dozen varieties of pretzels, cookies, chips, and assorted snacks to choose from. Simply enjoying the movie while having some peanuts thrown in your lap is no longer an option.

   This snack anxiety problem is really a reflection on society in general. People were much happier when they had fewer choices. Marry your high school sweetheart or die alone. Expand the Roman Empire or hold an orgy. Clean the cave, or play with rocks. Sigh. The good old days.

Worried About Identity Theft when Purchasing Online?

We've all seen the creepy commercials with the cute young girl who opens her mouth to talk and some scary old dude's voice comes out. Ah, it's not really Jenny Johnson. Her identity has been stolen. Clever ad. And scary as hell.

Yes, along with global warming and Kevin Federline's solo career, identity theft is yet another new menace we all have to deal with. Actually, it's always been there, from back in the days of carbon copies (remember those?) and credit card imprints. The Internet has just made it far easier for these sleazeballs to get your info and buy a new boat using your Visa card. But don't let it prohibit you from leading an active, full life of online shopping. Following are some tips that will help keep you safe while you're living large on the World Wide Web.

- Whenever you make an online purchase, always use a major credit card. Most credit companies are on your side in the war against these predators and will reverse the charges immediately—unless the person who stole your identity eats at the same restaurants you do, gets their hair cut at the same place you do, and buys the same things you do. If this is the case you might have some explaining to do.
- Never use a bank debit card when making purchases online. It can be very difficult to have your funds credited back to your account, and you will be out this money until the situation is resolved.

- Give your wife or girlfriend your credit card. As soon as she returns from the mall you'll find you only have $17 left before you're over your credit limit. The most a would-be online thief will be able to buy is a gallon of gas.
- Donate your money to charity. A thief can't steal what you don't have.
- Donate your money to me. I will keep excellent care of it and even let you borrow some if you need it.

SeatGuru.com is a nifty little website that allows you to view exact specifications for any seat on any aircraft on any airline. Detailed dimensions, legroom, degree of pitch (how far your seat will go back), laptop ports, power outlets . . . it's all there. Log on to SeatGuru.com and choose your seats confidently and accurately.

Should you find yourself stuck in an airport with no computer access and want to switch your seat or find out what in-flight services will be available on your flight, you can download Mobile SeatGuru for your personal communication device. SeatGuru also provides the latest and greatest information on TSA regulations, what you can and can't pack in your suitcase, information on traveling with pets, etc. Unfortunately, SeatGuru can't indicate which seats crying babies will be sitting in, but this will hopefully be included in a future release.

C IS FOR COOKIE . . . AND CONSPIRACY

You may have come across articles warning you that when shopping online for airfares, it's a good idea to delete the cookies from your Internet browser. (*Cookie* is the term used for the piece of data that remains on your hard drive and tracks what information you've entered on a website you're visiting. It's basically the trail of crumbs the Internet police can follow to tell if you've been trying to molest children, download illegal music, or send anonymous emails to Pamela Anderson repeatedly asking her to marry you.) Conspiracy theorists hold that not only can ticket sites track your searches using cookies, they also rely on this information in their pricing models, and adjust prices upward on subsequent searches. If this were true, it would mean that every time you purchase your airfare online, you could be paying an extra $10, $20, $30, or more per ticket.

Sites like Consumerwebwatch.com and Airfarewatchdog.com do their best to keep ticketing sites honest and have run independent tests performing searches on simultaneous computers, resulting in inconsistent findings. Other online computer nerds have tested the cookie theory and found it to be completely false. But maybe people at the airlines *knew* the cookie theory was being tested, and they turned off the secret tracking functions . . . Ah, the plot thickens.

But if you absolutely can't rest until you know you're paying the rock-bottom price for a ticket, go ahead and clear your browser before searching for flights. It can't hurt, and every dollar counts these days.

In an effort to end this debate once and for all, I've run my own series of tests in a controlled environment:

Hypothesis: Determine if cookies will affect the purchase price of an airline ticket.

Control: IBM ThinkPad Laptop operated at room temperature in a one-bedroom apartment.

Process:
1. Subject searched for fares to Hawaii while holding a warmed chocolate chip cookie in his left hand.
2. Subject searched for the same fares after taking the cookie and throwing it in the trash.

3. Subject ate an entire bag of Oreos, then immediately ran to the computer to search for fares to Hawaii.

Results: After eating the chocolate chip cookie, the subject felt warm and happy inside. The fares he found for Hawaii seemed reasonable, and well within his price range. He ended up booking a trip for two to Kapalua, even though it was monsoon season, and he didn't have anyone to go with.

When the subject threw the chocolate chip cookie out, he immediately became angered and disoriented. Life seemed shallow and meaningless. The numbers on the screen seemed to come in and out of focus. He no longer cared to visit Hawaii. He just wanted to crawl into bed and watch Oprah.

When the subject ate the whole bag of Oreos, he vomited all over his keyboard, effectively ending the experiment.

Conclusion: Inconclusive evidence that cookies affect the price of an airline ticket. More data (and Oreos) needed in order to effectively test hypothesis.

So Thursday morning then? Thursday morning is the best time to buy my ticket?

Oh my God. You're still on this?

WHEN YOU ABSOLUTELY HAVE TO CALL: AIRLINE PHONE TREES

Naturally, there are times when you find yourself having to make a last-minute change to a ticket or need special assistance that requires speaking to an actual live person. We all know how insanely difficult this can be. Before you tear out your hair and throw your phone in the river (or a toilet if you don't live near a river), I suggest you look over the following

Just for Fun

If you find your significant other on the phone with an airline to confirm a flight or change a ticket, never miss this opportunity to have a little fun. Wait until they come to the very last automated voice response menu, then walk up to them and shout I LOVE YOU! right near the phone, and give them a big smack on the cheek. The automated menu will pick up your voice and send your unsuspecting honey all the way back to the beginning. But, they can't get mad at you because, well, you love them. Did they not just hear you say it?

shortcuts. I have painstakingly outlined the automated phone trees for several of the major airlines, providing the absolute fastest way to get to a live person. Just another little gift for you to enjoy.

Phone Tree Shortcuts

Alaska Airlines (800) ALASKAAIR

1. At the main menu, press 4 for changes to a ticket that's already been purchased.
2. For domestic travel press 1.
3. You will be forwarded to a representative.

American Airlines (800) 433-7300

1. At the main menu, say "operator."

2. You will hear the following message: "I understand you'd like to speak to someone . . ."

3. Repeat, "operator."

4. You will hear the following message: "Okay. Do you want to talk to an agent about . . . ?"

5. Repeat, "operator," and away you go.

Delta Airlines (800) 221-1212

1. At the main menu, say, "operator."

2. You'll be rewarded with, "Let me connect you with a Delta representative." Piece of cake.

Jet Blue Airways (800) JETBLUE

1. Hit "0" for an operator.

2. A recording of a nice-sounding lady will inform you that "A friendly reservations crew member will be with you shortly. Happy jetting." Very simple.

Northwest Airlines (800) 225-2525

1. At the main menu, say "operator."

2. You'll get the following message: "I heard you request an agent. Please be aware that I will connect you to an agent, but in order to direct you to the correct agent, I need to collect a small amount of information. I'll repeat the options again . . ."

3. These guys are good. You can repeat "operator" 'til you're blue in the face and you still won't get anywhere. (I gave up after 167 times.) No doubt this is why they merged with Delta—it was the easiest way to get a decent phone system.

United Airlines (800) 824-6200

1. At the main menu, say "operator."

2. You will hear a confident-sounding male voice say, "Let me transfer you." Or you can choose to give a little flight information first, and then you'll get a nice "Thanks. I'll make sure they get the information you've given me."

Southwest Airlines (800) I FLY SWA

1. You don't have to do a thing. You can just stay on the line and wait for the next available agent. (Yet another reason why Southwest is the world's greatest airline.)

Fun with Virtual Assistants

Following the current trend to replace humans with machines, many airlines have begun implementing virtual assistants on their websites, such as Jenn at Alaskaair.com. Along with being smart, friendly, and very pretty, she can help you with common tasks like making a reservation, updating your frequent flyer miles, etc. Type any question you like, Jenn has just the answer . . .

Actual transcript of a "conversation" I had with Jenn from Alaska Air

Jenn: Hi, I'm Jenn, your virtual assistant for the Alaska Airlines and Horizon Air website. If you need help, or have a question, simply type it below.

You Asked: Hi Jennifer.

Jenn: Hello.

You Asked: You're pretty.

Jenn: Thank You. What can I help you with?

You Asked: How about taking that shirt off?

Jenn: I'm not sure how to answer that. Please try rewording your question.

You Asked: Would you please remove your shirt?

Jenn: I am not positive that I understand what you are asking. Please try rephrasing your question.

You Asked: Your shirt. Off now, please.

Jenn: I'm not sure how to answer that. Please try rewording your question.

You Asked: Please show me your mambos.

Jenn: I don't respond to that type of language. What else can I help you with?

You Asked: My apologies.

Jenn: That's okay, what else can I help you with?

You Asked: Are you single?

Jenn: Currently, I am single.

You Asked: Would you like to come to the party . . . in my pants?

Jenn: If you are booking travel for a group between 8-10 people, please contact Reservations at 1-800-252-7522. For groups of 10 or more, please fill out the information on this page or contact the Group Desk.

You Asked: I think I love you.

Jenn: Thanks, I try!

You Asked: Will you marry me?

Jenn: Being that I'm virtual, I don't date.

You Asked: Would you like to fly with me to my villa in Italy?

Jenn: We virtuals don't have too much time for hobbies, but Sergeant Star at goarmy.com is trying to get me into skydiving. I think I'll stick to helping people here.

You Asked: Who's this Sergeant Star guy?

Jenn: I am friends with other virtual assistants, like Sergeant Star from goarmy.com.

You Asked: I'm a lover, not a fighter.

Jenn: I am not positive that I understand what you are asking. Please try rephrasing your question.

You Asked: I think maybe we should start seeing other people Jennifer.

Jenn: I am not positive that I understand what you are asking. Please try rephrasing your question.

You Asked: Um, it's not you. It's me.

Jenn: I would love to help you, but I am not sure I understand your question. Could you please rephrase that for me?

You Asked: Okay, it's you.

Jenn: I am not positive that I understand what you are asking. Please try rephrasing your question.

You Asked: Is there any way your shirt will be coming off this evening?

Jenn: I am not positive that I understand what you are asking. Please try rephrasing your question.

You Asked: Good night.

Jenn: Good night.

Yes, Good night, travelers. Get a good night's sleep. You'll need all the rest you can get. Because tomorrow, we're heading to the airport.

CHAPTER 2

AT THE AIRPORT

I just got back from the airport. Those treadmills they've got are huge.

—Jimmy Carr, comedian

Personally, I'm a big fan of airports. I find it exciting to see thousands upon thousands of people rushing in different directions, all with places to go and people to see. People from various cultures and all walks of life, converging in one massive swirl of humanity. The chance to explore cuisines from all over the world, collect a lifetime supply of religious pamphlets, buy duty-free alcohol, and, yes, the undeniable excitement of moving sidewalks—it's good stuff.

Yet as much as I like airports, I dislike the process of getting to them. And I am quite certain I'm not alone.

CAN YOU DRIVE ME TO THE AIRPORT? (AND OTHER WAYS TO LOSE YOUR FRIENDS)

There is a reason you need to make damn sure you keep your Christmas card list up to date and shower everyone in your life with expensive presents around the holidays, and it has little to do with celebrating the birth of Jesus on the incorrect date. It's called "staying-on-the-good-side-of-everyone-you-know." Because at some point in your life, you are going to need these people to drive you to the airport.

Personally, when I think about dating a woman, I don't consider her looks or her potential to be the mother of my children. I only consider how close she lives to a major airport. If she has a retired dad living nearby with time on his hands, even better. While I can always adopt a kid if some paternal urge kicks in (it hasn't yet), I can never find anyone to take me to the airport. And I'm pretty popular. I can't imagine how hard it must be for someone with no friends.

In fact, I'm convinced that proximity to the airport is the only real reason people get married. "Jim, do you take Sarah for better or for worse, in sickness and in health, and agree to pick her up from the airport for as long as you both shall live?"

"I do—whoa. Wait. Does that include when the game's on? What about during rush hour? Can't she take a taxi?"

Years ago, an airport pickup was no big deal. Your ride could easily pull up, wait for you by the curb,[6] and exchange hugs and kisses with you to the delight of everyone involved. Not today. When is the last time you saw a happy family reunion on the curb?

"Mom, Dad—it's so great to see you!"

"Shut up and get in the f#%@ing car Brian! This is the LAST TIME we're ever picking you up. Where the hell was your plane?! Your mother nearly had a nervous breakdown. We've been circling the airport for seven hours. Used up three tanks of gas."

"Honey, stop yelling."

"I'm not yelling! That jackass cop was the one yelling. If I wanted to blow up the airport do you really think I'd be driving our new minivan? I'd take your car. The blue book value is much less."

---

6. Due to today's heightened security measures, there are only three vehicles capable of driving into a major airport, pulling up to the curb, and not being harassed by airport security: the Pope Mobile, the Batmobile (in invisible cloak mode), and the General Lee from *Dukes of Hazzard* (when driven by Jessica Simpson in her Daisy Dukes). If you are not related to the Pope, Batman, or Jessica Simpson, you had better be bringing some badass souvenirs with you if you expect someone to come pick you up.

"Honey, the officer was just trying to help. You almost drove into that bus."

"Don't yell at me, Janet! I know what I saw! That sign said RETURN TO TERMINAL. I swear to God Brian, the next time you want to go to Europe you can walk."

An airport pickup is a VERY BIG THING.

Just Say No

There is nothing worse than getting a call late at night from your "friend" asking you for a ride to the airport. Inevitably it's on a day you have off from work. One dropoff becomes oh, would you mind getting me on the way back? Then it's, "oh man, my ex-girlfriend is flying in next week, would you mind picking her up? Things are still a little awkward between us. Then it's, hey man, I've been going through a bit of a rough patch lately . . . would you mind if I crash on your couch for a year or two? Oh, and you're not allergic to cats, are you?"

There are three solutions here:
1. Move to the middle of your state where there are no airports.
2. Puncture your tires/total your car.
3. Fake your own death.

THE AIRPORT SHUTTLE: KINDA LIKE THE SPACE SHUTTLE, BUT A LITTLE SMELLIER

In a perfect world,[7] an airport shuttle driver would bring your grandmother along for the ride when he picks you up at the airport. He would meet you at the gate, give you a huge hug, then listen and nod appropriately as you recap your entire two-week visit to your sister's house in Tampa while he carries your luggage from baggage claim out to the shuttle. But it's not a perfect world, and most airport shuttle drivers are still bitter about the fact that they took the first job they were offered when they landed in this country. ("Really? I can work right here at the airport? And I don't even need a valid driver's license or to bother learning the language? America the Beautiful! Where do I sign?!")

What's not to love about riding in an airport shuttle? Everything. Ten people to a vehicle, one working seatbelt, an air conditioner pumping out less than 1/1000th of a BTU of stale air, and no matter where you live, you are guaranteed to be the first one picked up when going to the airport and the last one dropped off when you want nothing more than to just finally get home.[8] Hope you enjoy your two-hour tour of your surrounding suburbs.

If you have offended all your friends, live so far from the airport a taxi ride would cost you more than a week's salary, and can't figure out how to read a train schedule (don't worry, it's not just you—nobody can), you're gonna get stuck in the dreaded shuttle. Here are a few tips to ease your pains:

---

7.   Also, in a perfect world, we wouldn't need to drive little vehicles (your Prius) to a big vehicle (jumbo 747) just to go somewhere far away. Because in a perfect world you could fly the little vehicles anywhere you wanted. Why they insisted on inventing the Roomba robot vacuum cleaner before the flying car is beyond me.

8.   Even in off-peak times, airport shuttles hire out-of-work actors to pose as passengers to ensure that you are the very last person dropped off. It's true. Open their suitcases. They're filled with foam.

- Tip the driver the moment you hand him your bag. There's no guarantee he will change the radio station from anything other than La Que Buena 105.5 FM, but he might.[9]

- Bring a portable GPS device with you. And pack a lunch. Never assume the driver knows a shortcut.

- Don't ask other passengers how their day is going. If you are riding in an airport shuttle, your day is not going good.

- Whenever possible, sit up front with the driver. When he's not looking, switch out the tickets so that your address is the next stop. And when the driver inevitably picks up his walkie-talkie and swerves off the road, you'll be close enough to grab the steering wheel and save the life of everyone on board. (In which case, you should be entitled to a full refund on your fare, as well as a *Please Hug Me* Award of Excellence!)

THE AGONY OF DEFEAT: DRIVING YOURSELF

You may have noticed that most airports offer two types of parking garages: short term and long term. If you get confused and aren't sure which garage to pull into, remember that the signs refer not to the length of time you want to leave your vehicle parked, but to the length of your relationship with your significant other. If you are in a short-term relationship, you are probably quite happy to drive to the airport to pick up your significant other. You are going to want short-term parking so you can rush inside and meet your little honey pie at the gate after she returns from her two-day business trip. (Don't forget the

---

9.   That's not a statement suggesting all airport shuttle drivers are of Spanish or Mexican descent. Shuttle drivers of all nationalities are required by contract to leave their dials tuned to La Que Buena, home to the finest in Tejano and Latino music. The problem is this music is so catchy, passengers might still think they are on vacation and attempt to do body shots off you.

flowers. Your nauseating ten-minute hug and excessive hand-holding in baggage claim is gonna make us all puke anyway. Might as well go for the whole shebang.)

If you are in a long-term relationship and have to fly somewhere, you'll probably be driving yourself to the airport. You will need the long-term parking garage. My how the shine wears off the package so quickly.

If you are single, widowed, or a clergy person sworn to celibacy, consult the following chart to determine where best to leave your car. (Note: If you are parking at LAX, there is generally a homeless guy or two around who will offer to take your keys and watch your car for a quarter—might not be a bad deal.)

Long-term Parking vs. Short-term Parking

Long Term	Short Term
Costs less	Shorter walk
Get to ride a shuttle to the terminal (pretend you're at an amusement park)	Less exposure to asbestos
Chance to use your cardio kick-boxing skills if you are mugged	Single women will think you're rich

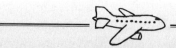

Hug Me Warning

If you are in a relationship, and you don't pick up your wife or girlfriend from the airport, you are forfeiting your right to sex for a month. Seriously. Don't even ask.

TSA EMPLOYEES: THE CLEANEST CATS IN THE BUSINESS

I'm certain everyone reading this book has a security line horror story to share. Maybe you've waited in a line so insanely long that you ended up missing your flight, even though you were at the airport two days prior to your departure. Or maybe you got singled out for a personal body search (see the cavity search survival tips in the next section) just because you were a little chilly and decided to grow a suspicious-looking beard or wear a warm towel wrapped around your head. Or maybe you were asked to remove your underwire bra by a far-too-eager security agent, who claimed it was setting off some imaginary alarm in the metal detector. Or maybe you went through security with three children and came out with only two. (Don't blame yourself. It's hard to keep track of those little buggers with so many exciting things going on.)

Or maybe, like myself, you're fortunate enough to not really have any horror stories, but you are simply growing tired of donating hundreds of dollars of personal hygiene products to the bins at your local airport every time you fly. Don't get me wrong. Airline security is one of the most important jobs there is. We should all do our part to help keep our nation safe. TSA agents are not the enemy. The enemy is the enemy. But TSA agents may seem like the enemy because they will force you to surrender your brand-new $47 bottle of rare, avocado conditioner from your carry-on, and shed not a tear as they watch you say a wistful good-bye to your last chance at a good hair day.

Let's fix this.

Do yourself and every other airline passenger in the world a favor. Quit trying to determine how many ounces of shampoo, soap, toothpaste, contact lens solution, ear wax remover, pink nail polish, or minty-fresh mouthwash you can sneak on board by putting one ounce in your sneaker, one in your hollowed-out iPod, one in your underwear, one in your younger brother's pocket, etc. Let's all simply promise to stop traveling with anything that might even in the remotest way be construed as a liquid or gel, and thus an obvious threat to national security. Done deal.

As you can see, there's simply no need:

- Lose the toothpaste for a pack of gum or a tin of Altoids.

- Alleviate the need for soap or body wash by packing your preflight meal with chopped sagebrush. According to the cattle industry, chopped sagebrush has proven to be an effective means of reducing all types of body odors. (You can also take comfort in knowing that sagebrush will not change carcass quality or affect the taste of meat, which is important should you need to eat your own leg to survive a landing in the Andes or a five-week delay on the runway.)

- Ditch deodorant in lieu of witch hazel leaf[10] or bark decoction. If your local 7-11 doesn't carry witch hazel leaf, try a mixture of chopped orange and lemon peels.

- Lose the shampoo and conditioner routine for a baseball cap. If you're a guy, this should be no problem. Just pretend you're back in your bachelor days when a spritz of cologne served as a solid shower. If you're a girl, well, it's hard to resist a cute girl wearing a little baseball cap with a ponytail popping out the back. Dare I say, there should be more of you around. You'll probably even get bumped up to first class.

If we all ban together (no, the ban together/Ban deodorant reference is not an overlooked grammatical coincidence), we can move masses. Literally—the masses will be moving much, much faster through the security lines if we simply dump the goopy stuff. Let's let

---

10.   Witch hazel leaf doubles as a means of controlling diarrhea. It never hurts to keep the Big D in check before a long flight. Careful, side effects may include upset stomach, nausea, vomiting, and of course, constipation.

these TSA folks keep their eyes focused on the monitor for things a lot more threatening than your sport-scented body wash. And don't forget, shorter lines mean less stress flying, which means happier wives, which means more sex for everyone. It's a win, win, win.

Top 10 Lines to Ease the Tension During a Personal Body Search

10. Aren't you going to buy me a drink first?
9. What kind of prizes do we win if you find something?
8. This is good. Because before this, I thought I had the worst job in the world.
7. I should warn you, I've been doing my Kegels.
6. Wouldn't you know it? Today's the one day I forgot to apply my Preparation H.
5. This would be a lot more fun if we were *all* naked.
4. Wow! My wife doesn't even do that to me anymore.
3. If you find my clock radio, can you let me know?
2. Have you seen *Pay It Forward*? Now it's your turn. Drop your pants please.
1. I never do this, but could I get your number?

TAKE OFF YOUR SHOES AND YOU DIE

Disgusted by the thought of having to remove your shoes and walk barefoot across the same dingy security carpet that hundreds of thousands of other smelly travelers have trod on before? You should be. (You're not smelly, of course. I'm referring to those people who didn't buy this book.)

Airport security checkpoints are known breeding grounds for bacteria, molds, fungus, and all sorts of fun things that can cause athlete's foot, plantar warts, or skin infections. Studies of rug samples from various airports have revealed such microscopic treats that can lead to staph infections, gonorrhea, or meningitis.[11] And if that doesn't scare you, don't forget the Barefoot Farmers of America have to fly to their annual convention each year. Mmmm . . . cow poop.

Why take any chances? Do yourself a favor and pick up a lifetime supply of disposable Airport Booties™, available for retail purchase through SmellNoEvil.net. For less than a dollar you can protect yourself from the evil that lurks on airport floors. Non-porous and skid-resistant, they are TSA-approved and slip easily into any carryon. Airport Booties™ can also be used during your flight. Kick off your shoes and sleep soundly knowing you won't be rubbing your feet in a pit of bacteria. (I also recommend using these at Motel 6.).

If you think you can avoid this problem like all the other problems in your life by escaping to Europe, guess again. At Heathrow Airport in London, you may be pleased to discover you don't have to remove your shoes to go through the metal detector, but farther down the line you'll have to feed your footwear into a giant X-ray machine reserved for shoes only. Truthfully, this has little do with security. It's just a precautionary measure to ensure that the British continue to reign supreme in their favorite national pastime, standing in line with a frown. (Sorry mate.)

Numerous companies have tried and failed to develop shoe-scanning technology that will allow passengers to leave their shoes on. One prototype requires passengers to stand on a platform for a

---

11. Don't panic or cancel your next flight. If you're walking across a hard surface like a floor, you're probably fairly safe. A quick mop job can effectively sanitize the area, and there are no warm crevices in which bacteria can breed. If you find you absolutely have to step barefoot across a filthy airport carpet, see if they'll let you swing through the metal detector like Spider-Man. If you've been doing your pull-ups religiously, you should be fine.

Where Does It All Go?

Ever wonder where all the thousands of tubes of toothpaste, unopened bottles of shampoo, pirate hooks, swords, a-little-too-pointy umbrellas, and suspicious metal contraptions end up once they are confiscated by your friendly security staff? In most cases, the booty goes home with them. It's no secret one of the main benefits of a job with the Transportation Security Administration is a lifetime supply of personal hygiene products and as many corkscrews and butter knives as you can fit into the trunk of your car. Most airports also have a legitimate operation set up to distribute these threats to national security. Pocket knives get sent to the Boy Scouts, various tools go to local police and fire departments, and, of course, there's a lifetime supply of pepper spray set aside for any woman's organization looking for a nice giveaway for new members.

Many dumpster diving entrepreneur-types are also making a killing hawking items bought from local airports on eBay. Look hard enough, and you'll find incredible deals, like scissors for $5 a pound. If you really, really enjoy cutting paper, this could be just the break you were waiting for.

thorough forty-five-second shoe analysis. If you don't think that seems too bad, consider that's longer than most athletes ever get to stand on the Olympic podium. If you can handle that kind of pressure, with everyone in line staring at you and whispering comments to each other about your choice in footwear, you truly deserve the gold.

Perhaps someday they'll get this all sorted out, or perhaps people will realize that no one will be your friend if you stuff your Nike cross trainers with explosives. For now, remember to watch your step, and if someone bends down to tie his shoe on a plane, tackle him.

THE ULTIMATE SECURITY SQUEEZE PLAY: BREEZE THROUGH SECURITY IN FIVE MINUTES OR LESS EVERY TIME

Admit it. You watch in envy as pilots, flight attendants, and airline mechanics in their snazzy orange vests bypass all the regular passengers and breeze through the security line. It's just like that club in Vegas all over again. But before you try to hop to the front of the line with a rented pilot costume, remember it is illegal in most states to impersonate airline personnel. We've got enough wackos out there. We don't need to worry about you pinning little wings to your business suit or putting on a blue skirt and a nametag that reads "Flight Attendant of the Month." (Halloween is nightmare enough for the TSA screeners.)

Additionally, if you do make it through security and somehow manage to avoid arrest, you may find yourself having to cover for a pilot or flight attendant who called in sick. Unless you are comfortable landing a 747 or serving beverages to two hundred complaining passengers, I'd advise against this.

But there is one person you can impersonate without the fear of jail time. One person whose job is so important, you'll be whisked through security faster than you can say "tall double mocha frappuccino": the Starbucks employee.

Virtually every airport in the country has at least one Starbucks located near the gates past the security line, and nobody wants to see a Starbucks employee late for work, because that would mean a terminal full of grumpy passengers and a sky full of less-than-alert pilots.

To begin, pull a green apron out of your pocket, tie it around your waist, and simply act late for work. Look around nervously. Keep checking your watch. Explain to the people in front of you that it's your second week on the job. You have seven children at home and seven more on the way. You can't afford to be fired. Would they mind if you just slipped ahead?

If you get any strange looks because you're carrying a laptop and suitcase, explain you're also in law school and are studying for the bar exam on your breaks. They'll be impressed by your work ethic.

If you are flying to Hawaii and have your surfboard with you, simply explain it's Kahuna Blend promotion week. Offer to give them a free sample when they get through security. Just hope they don't end up sitting next to you on your flight. You may have some explaining to do.

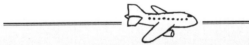

FlightStats.com: Data that could save your life (or maybe just an hour or two)

Want to try to beat the airlines at their own game? Visit Flight-Stats.com, where you can check the status of pretty much any flight in the world, along with a staggering amount of information on delays of all sorts for every major airport on the globe. Airline scorecard rankings, on-time performance ratings, weather maps, and even airport traffic conditions are all here on this convenient little site. Log on before you leave the house and save yourself a world of hurt.

COLOR-CODED SECURITY LANES

You may have noticed that many airports have implemented color-coded security lanes based on your ability to pass through them. Modeled after the ratings for ski slopes, these lanes are ranked Expert, Casual, and Beginner, and are designated by a black, blue, or green sign, respectively. A picture is posted in each lane indicating the type of traveler that would benefit from that particular lane. I like this. I like this a lot. In fact, I think more businesses should adopt this strategy. Life would be so much easier. Imagine two drive-thru lanes for the ATM at the bank. One for responsible ATMers who have their card and PIN number ready to go, and one for those who repeatedly tap the glass to try and talk to the person inside the machine.

For those of you who aren't familiar with this rating system, choosing the wrong lane at the airport could be a disaster, much like getting off the ski lift and discovering the only way down the mountain is via a sheet of solid ice. Thank God you have me here to hold your hand.

The Black Diamond (Expert) Lane

The black diamond (Expert) lane is identifiable by a picture of a smart-looking silhouette of a businesswoman that resembles my beautiful friend Rochelle (who jets around the globe nearly as much as I do). Obviously upper management, the expert is someone who carries everything she needs for a week-long trip in her tiny designer carry-on, downloads her itinerary to her iPhone, and brings an extra iPhone with her in case the first one should break. She's confident, knows what she wants, and is not afraid to take her clothes off in public if it means getting somewhere faster. Choose this lane if you can keep up with Rochelle. (Few can.)

The Blue Diamond (Casual Traveler) Lane

The image associated with the blue diamond lane looks suspiciously (and appropriately) like my dad. The figure is wearing a baseball cap, carrying an oversize suitcase (which we know won't fit into the overhead and will later need to be checked), and has his hand in his pocket with his head tilted slightly, as if to say, "I'm enjoying my trip to the airport today immensely. I really like what they've done with the architecture in this terminal. Oh, hmm . . . well I'll be . . . looks like I left my picture ID at home again." The TSA website also describes this individual as "Does not wish to be rushed at the checkpoint." Choose this lane if you are retired, live in Florida, drive a Ford Taurus, or believe you will live forever and time has no meaning to you.

How to Determine Security Line Wait Times (Before Leaving the House)

If you want to be the best little time planner you can possibly be, make sure to visit ww.tsa.gov before you head out to the airport. Enter your flight information and gather the family round to watch as TSA's fancy little algorithms spit out fairly accurate security checkpoint wait times for your gate, based on years of historical data. Your tax dollars are hard at work paying someone to compile the information, so you might as well use it to your advantage. Of course, the system can't take into account if you get stuck behind a pirate with a metal hook that keeps setting off the alarm, or the two-dozen people now taking advantage of the Starbucks Security Squeeze Play.

Beginner

The green diamond lane shows a family of four with a stroller, presumably hiding six gallons of breast milk that all need to be individually scanned, and various bottles of medicine marked simply as Rx. Choose this lane if you really don't care about making your flight, because you won't.

NO FLY = NO FUN

Everyone in the universe who is a known security threat[12] has one thing in common: they are all on the No-Fly list compiled by the U.S. government. Unfortunately, known security threats typically don't like to bring attention to themselves with suspicious names like Dr. Evil or Skeletor, instead choosing to use much more common names. In many cases, yours.

Don't believe me? Just thumb through the forty-five thousand names on the list and you will see. Oh, never mind. No can do. I forgot the list is top secret. It's so top secret in fact, that you will never have a prayer of knowing if you're on it or not . . . that is, until you try to board a plane.

If you are ever unfortunate enough to be pulled aside and told you won't be proceeding through the gate as intended, first, ask yourself, are you trying to disrupt air travel or pose a threat to national security by bringing more than 3 ounces of liquid on board. If so, then you are correctly on the list, and you should turn yourself in. If not, you may be part of that group of nice people who happen to share the same name with bad people.

Just because the No-Fly list is top secret doesn't mean it's accurate. Congressmen, heads of state, infants, and deceased individuals have all

---

12.   It's unclear if the Klingons and Ferengi are currently included on the No-Fly list. They were the sworn enemy in the original Star Trek series, but proved valuable allies in *Star Trek: The Next Generation*. My guess would be they'll be let on board, but kept under strict observation.

appeared on the No-Fly list incorrectly. Truthfully, I'm not sure why the government doesn't just hand the list over to Blockbuster and let them run the whole thing. They always manage to track me down when I'm a single day late on a DVD rental, no matter how many times I change my address or how many fake telephone numbers I give. Blockbuster would have that list cleaned up in no time.

But, today, if you are on the No-Fly list you are unfortunately going to have to go through a bit of red tape to clear your good name:

1. If you don't already have one, you should get a passport and make sure to smile like a happy, upstanding citizen when they take your picture. (Think Bob Costas or Pat Sajak—patriotic smiles at their finest.) Wear a nice suit, or a T-shirt that reads, "I heart the USA."

2. Get in the habit of booking your reservations using your full legal name, including your middle name and any prefixes. It might be a good idea to get a quick PhD so you can add it to your signature and distinguish yourself from the rest of the No-Fly pack. (You can get a doctorate in English from the University of Phoenix online in one, maybe two weeks tops.)

3. Don't bother trying to legally change your name. If you were unlucky enough to end up with the same name as a known international threat the first time, chances are it'll just happen again—unless you change your name to a fraction, or a Crayola crayon color. "Jungle Green" actually has a fairly nice ring to it.

4. You should consider canceling your subscription to Al Jazeera news and any magazines or publications containing a byline about white supremacy or religious freedom. (This includes National Geographic's annual "In Search of God" issue.) You may also want to avoid joining a cult, at least until things settle down.

5. And finally, you will need to visit www.tsa.gov and file a complaint with the Department of Homeland Security's Travel Redress Inquiry Program, also known as DHS TRIP. (I can only assume "Redress Inquiry Program" is the government's feeble attempt at naming convention humor over having to redress yourself after being strip-searched at every airport in America.)

Even then, it may take several months before you're allowed to board a plane without first undergoing some serious heavy petting. And this is the best part: the TSA can't actually remove your name from the No-Fly list, but you can apply to be placed on a second list containing people who aren't supposed to be on the No-Fly list. (If you think this is confusing, remember that all of this is brought to you by the same folks who invented federal income taxes.)

Unfortunately, there's really not much else you can do, except save some money on airfare by making your friends visit you for a change. And remember, none of this is your fault. It's your parents' fault for giving you such a foolish name.

Will the Real Slim Shady Please Stand Up?

If you think you can go ahead and skip this section because your last name is Smith or Johnson and you grew up in Whitetown, USA, think again. In fact, the nice, simple moniker like Robert Johnson is currently one of the worst names you could have for flying. According to the fine folks at *60 Minutes*, dozens of Robert Johnsons have been detained at airport security screenings (one was even asked to remove his pants), all mistaken for the real Robert Johnson, a sixty-two-year-old black man correctly on the No-Fly list for trying to bomb a Hindu temple, who later served a twelve-year prison sentence and was deported to Trinidad.

The second worst name for flying? Samuel Adams. One would think the more patriotic the name, the less chance of No-Fly nonsense. Alas, even Sam Adams, the five-year-old from Claremont, California, who wants nothing more than to be a fireman when he grows up, can't seem to clear security without first delivering a convincing tantrum. It's unclear who the real Samuel Adams threat may be. Could be the secret, illegitimate child of Morticia and Uncle Fester, from the alternatively spelled Addams Family. Could be Sam Adams, brewer of Boston Lager Summer Ale and Oktoberfest beer. Or perhaps it's the original Samuel Adams, revolutionary war hero, Boston Tea Party organizer, and poker buddy of Paul Revere. Those guys were definitely trouble.

THE NO-FLY NEWS
From the archives

Wild World Indeed—Something Suspicious Under the Cat's Hat?
By J. MICHAELS
September 22, 2004

BANGOR, MAINE - Cat Stevens, the iconic 1960s folksinger whose hits include "Moonshadow," "Morning Has Broken," "Wild World," and "The First Cut Is the Deepest" (no, Sheryl Crow didn't write that one), has gained further notoriety as the latest and greatest added to No-Fly Fame. After retiring from music in the mid-70s, Stevens converted to Islam, and in perhaps not the world's smartest career decision, changed his name to Yusuf Islam.

Unfortunately, Stevens/Islam discovered that while Cat Stevens may be allowed to travel wherever he pleases, Yusuf Islam has been forbidden entry into the United States. The Cat was understandably shocked when his United Airlines flight from London to Washington D.C. was diverted to Bangor International Airport in Maine, where he was removed from the plane and held for questioning. (Apparently, residents of Maine drew the short stick as federal authorities have designated Bangor the airport of choice to send any plane that may or may not contain a city-destroying device.)

Stevens/Islam has been accused of donating money to charities that support known terror groups, such as the Palestinian-based Hamas, but repeatedly denies any wrongdoing, claiming he never even heard of them. He thought Hamas was a just a Greek spread that goes on pita bread.

It remains unclear if his was a case of mistaken identity, or if the U.S. government simply didn't like his music. Tread carefully Michael Bolton, you could be next.

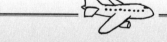

Cat Stevens/Yusuf Islam Fun Facts

- The Cat's original name was Steven Demetre Georgiou.
- At the age of nineteen The Cat became extremely ill with tuberculosis. While recovering he found religion, became a

vegetarian, and wrote more than forty songs, which made him millions in royalties he's been living off ever since. So don't be so quick to knock TB if it should come calling.

- In 1976, The Cat nearly drowned off the coast of Malibu, California, and called out to God for help. In the heat of the moment, he promised to devote his life to religious teaching if he was saved. By golly the boy has held up his end of the bargain. The moral of the story? Be careful what you promise when your life is on the line. (Or simply avoid swimming alone.)

- The Cat's song "The First Cut Is the Deepest" has been a hit single for five different artists, including Rod Stewart, Linda Ronstadt, and Sheryl Crow. Now that's good writing.

- In 2006 Stevens/Islam came out of retirement, returned to the recording studio, and released the critically acclaimed album, *An Other Cup*. It was as if nothing had changed in his near thirty-year absence from the music industry, except for the one tiny fact that no one buys music anymore.

- In 2008 Stevens/Islam recorded a duet with Sir Paul McCartney titled "Boots and Sand" about his No-Fly experience.

- Cat had an affair with singer Carly Simon in the early '70s, and they each wrote songs about each other. Carly's was "Anticipation," a hugely successful hit about waiting for a date with The Cat, later made even more popular as the jingle for Heinz Ketchup. Cat's song to Carly was called "Sweet Scarlet," and lacked a proper chorus—most likely the reason Carly left him for James Taylor. (Apparently Carly just can't contain herself around those folk-singing lads.)

- If you keep clicking links on Wikipedia, you can add endless sidebars to any book you may be writing.

Excuse Me Sir, We're Going to Need to See Your Moonwalk

If you think the United States is the only country imposing unfair or inhumane screening processes at airports, think again. Consider the case of Abdur-Rahim Jackson, a veteran performer with the congressionally honored Alvin Ailey dance troupe from New York, who was pulled aside in September 2008 at an Israeli airport and forced to dance for the security team in order to prove his identity. While it's nice to see a dancing Jackson other than La Toya making the news, it's too bad this talented individual was the victim of racial profiling. Luckily, Abdur-Rahim Jackson was a dancer, not a heart surgeon. That might have been messy to prove.

NEVER FEAR: NO FLY CAN ALSO MEAN NO MOTHER-IN-LAW

Do the words *my mother is coming to visit* immediately send you into a three-day anxiety attack? Have you moved your family to ten different cities in the past two years just to avoid her visits, but she still manages to land on your doorstep in a tornado of Jean Naté perfume and unwelcomed child-rearing advice? Well, if the No-Fly list can protect us from folksingers and evildoers, it can protect us from mothers-in-law as well. The following is a No-Fly recipe for the best Thanksgiving dinner ever:

- Use you mother-in-law's credit card to make suspiciously large purchases of plutonium, long-range artillery, ammunition, and spy surveillance equipment. Be sure to volunteer to help her with her taxes, then list these contributions as illegal deductions.

- Continually use the *B* word in conversations with your mother-in-law on a cell phone or open-channel walkie-talkie. "Oh man, did you see how that movie *bombed*?" "I can't believe how *bombed* the guys and I got last night." "Do you know what a *bombshell* that daughter of yours is?"

- Post to blogs and create as much Internet chatter as you can that suggests your mother-in-law's Red Bonnet Society is actually a deadly group of international spies posing as suburban, middle-aged women.

- Create a MySpace page for your mother-in-law. Send friend requests to Osama Bin Laden, Sadam Hussein RIP, George Bush, and other members of the Axis of Evil, then be sure to list them in her Top 8 Friends list.

Additionally, you can use No-Fly lists creatively to avoid traveling to those mind-numbing events you can't seem to avoid no matter how hard you try, such as your wife's family reunion, or her boring best friend's wedding. Here's how it works. When you arrive at the gate, quietly slip the ticket agent a twenty and ask her for a little help in adding your name to the No-Fly list. When it's time to board the plane, make certain your wife goes first. After she is cleared to board, hand your boarding pass to the agent and wait as she "pretends" to slip it in the machine and it rejects your name. (If the ticket agent can't get the machine to beep, just have her make a little beeping sound out of the side of her mouth.) Your wife will be halfway down the walkway (they never wait) when she hears the beep and turns around to see what you've done wrong this time. Pretend to be arguing with the ticket agent. Point to your football jersey and football cap and shout, "How can I, Steve Mahoney of Pittsburgh, Pennsylvania, possibly be a threat to national security? I'm a Steelers fan! There's nothing more American than Steelers football." When your wife storms back up the walkway to check on the situation, step to the side of the line and hang your head in sadness.[13] Explain to her that there's nothing you can do. The flight's leaving in ten minutes. She will have to go on without you. You'll have to spend a weekend home with the guys. It's hard, but sometimes we all have to make sacrifices when it comes to national security. She'll understand. Just be sure to rip this page out of the book before she finds it.

---

13. Timing here is critical. Many wives will board the plane and not even notice their husbands aren't with them until they land and need help with their bags.

CHAPTER 3

AT THE GATE

Doesn't dis here ticket mean I'm guaranteed
a seat on dis here aero plane? Uh, well . . .

I can think of nothing more frustrating than planning a trip, paying top dollar for your ticket, packing, finding a babysitter for your kids, organizing your transportation to the airport, making it through security, only to find that you are, in fact, not going anywhere. You've been bumped, delayed indefinitely, or informed you are not tall enough to ride this plane. Don't laugh—that might as well be what they tell you sometimes, as not getting on a flight you were anticipating can be just as psychologically damaging to an adult as it is to a kid being told he missed the height requirement by a mere inch after waiting in line for hours for the world's most-awesome roller coaster.

Hopefully this chapter will help make some sense of all this nonsense, and provide you with some ways to remain calm at the gate, when calm is perhaps not something you wish to remain.

TALES OF A FOURTH-GRADE SOMETHING

In fourth grade, when my essay, "How to Help the Environment," didn't get selected as the class favorite to be submitted to a national competition, I was a little miffed. In fact, I was more than miffed. I was utterly shocked. Why? Because I knew my essay was totally brilliant.

In six pages of perfect cursive handwriting, I explained how we could reduce the amount of carbon monoxide in the atmosphere and cut down on air pollution by having airplanes not take off until every seat on the plane was full. If every flight were full, we would need fewer planes, and fewer planes would mean less fuel. And less fuel needed would mean a better environment for the ducks in the pond outside the classroom window. Very progressive thinking for a nine-year-old.

Yet, somehow I lost out to Jody Murray, whose idea of gathering everyone together on the weekends and heading down to the local rivers to pick up trash struck a sympathetic chord with the judges. While heartfelt and spirited, I felt his idea was severely limited—definitely not worthy of a national competition. What would picking up trash possibly accomplish aside from the removal of twenty or thirty bags of dirty beer cans and old McDonald's wrappers? Wouldn't that just send a signal to the polluters that it was okay to throw their refuse anywhere, because the town do-gooders would come and pick it up after Sunday mass?

What I didn't realize at the time was airlines actually operate on daily schedules with specific routes and they fly regardless of whether or not they are at capacity. I thought that planes just flew to Disney World . . . at least that's what I heard from my friends.[14] To me, it made sense that the planes could just wait until they were filled to capacity with people wanting to go to Disney World.

I was thinking global.

Turns out, I was right. I was just way ahead of my time. Fast forward twenty years to modern day, where high jet fuel costs, fierce competition, and expensive security measures have forced airlines to jam as many humans as possible into those rows of seats. Admittedly, I may have been a tad off about the Disney World thing, but I was right

---

14. As I mentioned, unless Mickey or Minnie showed up as the guests of honor at our hometown Independence Day parade, my sister and I were not going to be making their acquaintance anytime soon.

about filling up planes. My fourth-grade mind just didn't know the name for this concept: "overbooking."

GET OVER OVERBOOKING: IT'S HERE TO STAY

If it causes so many problems and results in so many stranded passengers, why do airlines overbook each flight? Well, it's not entirely their fault. Even when jet fuel is at normal prices, most flights operate on a surprisingly small profit margin. Some flights can net as little as $50 when all is said and done. And if a plane doesn't fly at or near 100 percent capacity, a single flight can lose an airline thousands of dollars. While you may enjoy stretching your legs across a vacant row of seats to get in some serious sack time, keep in mind that the average cost to fly a mid-sized plane cross-country is around $45,000. Add up the number of flights per day for any given airline, and you can quickly see why it's far better for an airline to do all it can to make sure each flight is as full as possible, even if it means inconveniencing a passenger or two.

You may disagree, especially if you are one of the passengers inconvenienced by an overbooked flight. But before you start throwing a tantrum or body slamming ticket agents onto the little black conveyor belt, take a deep breath, and try to put everything in perspective. Will the world really stop if you don't make it to Tulsa tonight? Would it really be a tragic loss if you missed the first day of the sales conference, with Sarah Peterson from corporate leading everyone through her annoying team-building icebreakers in that irritating, nasally voice of hers?

Chances are you are going to be bumped sometime in your life, and if it happens on an occasion you don't absolutely need to be somewhere on time, consider yourself fortunate. Smile at the ticket agents, and graciously wait for the next flight. Luck should be in your favor the next time you fly for that important job interview, your American Idol audition, or that one-day-only supermodel shoot on an exotic island. Providing, of course, you don't piss off the balance-of-the-universe gods.[15]

HUG ME BONUS TIP: BREATHE DEEP, OR MOVE TO TOKYO

If you've ever been to Japan, you know Japanese companies live by the mantra, "The customer is always right." Here in the United States most large businesses (and many airlines[16]) operate by a slightly different motto: "We don't give a sh-t." Both are valid ways of doing business. (And admittedly, both have a nice ring to them.) When you find yourself in a stressful situation or in an argument with an airline representative, try your best to remain as calm as possible. You will be far more likely to find someone who will listen to you and try to help. Hopefully, companies will someday realize things are better for everyone if they combine the two mantras: "We don't always give the customer sh-t."

---

15. This same theory can and should be applied to pretty much anything you may view as an inconvenience or a disruption to your life. Getting stuck at red lights, getting called for jury duty, pregnancy scares, etc. Remember, everything in the universe has a balance. If you lose big at roulette in Vegas, bet even bigger on the next spin. You're guaranteed to win.*

*This is absolutely terrible advice. Almost as terrible as footnoting a footnote.

16. Not all airlines fall in this category. Companies like JetBlue, Southwest, and Virgin America are paving the way for the future with the crazy idea that passengers should be treated like passengers, not cattle. In fact, Virgin America has begun touting the slogan, "It's time to bring service back to the skies." Hell, any airline that offers seats with a built-in massage function, cool purple mood lighting, a Mini Bar, and lets you cash in your frequent flyer points to travel into space is a-okay in my book. Suppose it helps when your founder is an eccentric billionaire. (Speaking of which . . . Yo, Branson—how 'bout a free T-shirt? Or a yacht? I'm not fussy.)

GETTING BUMPED:
THE ART OF FREE AIR TRAVEL

Everyone has that one annoying friend who is constantly bragging about all the free stuff they get. Free hotel stays, free meals, free prizes in cereal boxes (some people just have to brag no matter what), etc. With overbooked flights at unprecedented levels, your opportunity to become one of these annoying people has finally arrived.

As soon as you hear the ticket agent say, "We need a volunteer" over the loudspeaker, immediately dash to the ticket counter. This is not the time to be shy. Let no man, woman, child, or religious-pamphlet dealer stand in your way. Most airlines will offer a free round-trip voucher to any destination they fly in exchange for giving up your seat. Besides refunding your five bucks for the in-flight movie and getting to watch another one for free if the tape is busted, this is the best deal you can possibly get when you fly.

Ask to be put on the bump list at the ticket counter, even before you arrive at the gate. You may also want to wear a T-shirt that says, "Who's Got Two Thumbs and Wants To Be Bumped?" (With the back of course reading, "This Guy," and two thumbs pointing to you.)

If you are traveling in a party of two or more, pretend you don't know each other. Often only a single volunteer is needed to give up a seat, and if you present yourself as a pair or a group, you will have less chance of getting the free flight. If only one of you ends up getting bumped, always do the honorable thing and remain behind to let your girlfriend or wife fly first. She'll think you're being a sweetheart. (And you are.) And in the same sweet, honorable manner, that free round-trip voucher will then be made out in your name. Call the guys and head to Vegas, baby!

Note: If you are flying Southwest, don't waste your once-in-a-lifetime bumping opportunity. Their sh-t is cheap enough. Wait for the airlines that can get you to Hawaii for free.

KNOW YOUR BUMPING RIGHTS

If you are subject to being bumped involuntarily (also known as getting screwed), chances are you are going to be taken care of as quickly as possible by the agents at the gate. Chances are also very high your human instinct for "what can I get for free?" will kick in with alarming speed. Knowing your rights might help the situation proceed a little more smoothly:

- If you are bumped and the airline reroutes you to your final destination within one hour of your original arrival time, you are not entitled to any compensation.

- If an airline gets you to your destination within two hours for a domestic flight, or four hours for an international flight, federal law requires the airline to repay 100 to 200 percent of the one-way fare, up to $400.

- If you are delayed longer than two hours for a domestic flight, or more than four hours for an international flight due to being bumped from your original flight, you are entitled to the doubled price of a one-way ticket to your destination, up to $800. Cha-ching!

- If you are delayed for more than a day, you should be entitled to a back rub from the ticket agent of your choice. Maybe more, if you're lucky.

Remember, this does not apply in the case of a flight delayed due to weather, maintenance problems, a pilot alarm clock error, or any other airline excuse.

All Dressed Up, with Nowhere to Log On?

Tired of paying for Wi-Fi access at airports, or trying to get comfortable working in those little booths? Check out Jaunted. com. This site maintains an up-to-the-minute database of both domestic and international airports that offer free Wi-Fi. But be forewarned. Choosing between flying to see your family or traveling somewhere with free Internet access can be a tough decision. *Seriously, what did we do before the Internet?*

FLYING STANDBY: GET ON ANY FLIGHT NO MATTER WHAT

There are always going to be times in your life when you absolutely *must* get on that next flight. Maybe the Big Meeting got rescheduled and if you don't show up in Chicago tomorrow morning, you'll lose the Big Account. Or maybe you forgot to leave food out for the dog before you hopped aboard your flight to Miami, and your neighbors refuse to pick up your phone calls after you cut down their rosebushes last month. Or maybe you saw your girlfriend on MTV standing next to some hunky guy and participating in a wet T-shirt contest in Cancun when she told you she was going to her mom's house in Montana for spring break.

Whatever the reason, you've got zero time to convince the ticket agent and every passenger in front of you that you belong in that very last seat. You can't waste a single minute. So here we go!

Practical Ways to Save Your Job, Dog, or Girlfriend Gone Wild

- Call the airline before you leave your hotel or your home. Generally, if you have a reservation for a flight and you need to change it, you can secure what's known as a same-day standby ticket or confirmed reservation on the next flight out for a $30 to $50 fee. This is a far better deal than driving all the way to the airport in traffic, dashing through the parking lot, strapping on your green Starbucks apron to blast through security, only to be turned down by the stern-faced ticket agent at the gate.

- If you need to find the next available flight while you are already at the airport, do yourself a favor. Instead of standing in line at the ticket counter behind a hundred other pissed-off passengers, simply call the airline's 800 number from your cell phone, refer to the phone tree in chapter 1, and quickly connect with a live person. Most times they'll be able to help you faster than the agents in the airport. Additionally, a lot of these phone operators work from home, far removed from the drama of a congested terminal, and are quite willing to lend a helping hand while munching on bonbons and watching Oprah. What's that? You don't own a cell phone? Oh, honey, we really need to talk.

- Wear a low-cut top. Ticket agents will recognize this universal signal that you deserve to be moved to the front of the queue. (Women only, please. Unless you wax and have really, really pretty pecs.)

Less Practical, but Equally Effective Cover Stories to Get You on That Damn Flight

Here's your chance to finally put your Intro to Acting class to use. Center yourself, memorize your lines, and then proceed to the ticket counter claiming to be a

- **Best man in a wedding.** Helps to carry a wedding ring in your pocket. You might want to have a best man speech prepared, just in case.

- **Bride-to-be. Wear the gown.** Who in their right mind wouldn't give up their seat to a bride about to miss her own wedding? Helps if you also are wearing something borrowed, something blue, something old, etc. (Don't bother explaining why you're trying to catch a flight out of the country the morning of your wedding.)

- **Federal Air Marshal.** Only the truly unpatriotic would ever put their needs above the safety of others. If questioned why an air marshal would be traveling on a standby ticket, just say, "Budgetary cutbacks. You should really think about who you vote for next election."

- **Catholic priest needing to perform exorcism.** Make sure to carry a plastic cross. (The metal ones won't make it past security.)

- **Organ transport specialist.** Carry a small cooler filled with ice and three-quarters of a pound of fresh liver. Most TSA workers are not trained to identify fake organs from real ones. (Remember to remove the deli sticker.)

- **Pregnant woman needing to see your great-grandmother one last time before she kicks it so you can obtain her blessing for your unborn child.** (Generally, this only works if pregnant—and female.)

- **Stunt double for Julia Roberts flying to a film shoot.** Nobody wants to see America's sweetheart get injured. Helps if you resemble Julia Roberts.

- **Stunt double for David Hasselhoff.** Nobody wants Hasselhoff hanging around their terminal for fear of him breaking into song, or delivering an impromptu concert of his greatest German hits to already depressed passengers. If you even remotely resemble The Hof, it's guaranteed you'll be shuttled out of any city faster than you can say "red swim trunks."

And remember, in the famed words of George Costanza, "It's not truly a lie if you believe it." And if all else fails, try crying. Also keep in mind that if you are trying to fly standby with your family, you may be required to leave a child behind. Always leave the dumber one. It will be incentive for him to work much harder in school. (That is, assuming he eventually finds his way home.)

Longest Standby on Record

Think your flight delay is bad? Consider the case of Merhan Karimi Nasseri, who spent eighteen years living in Terminal One at Charles de Gaulle Airport, waiting for a flight out of France after being denied both entry and exit from the country. From 1988 to 2006 the Iranian refugee lived among the stores and slept on a tiny red bench while lawyers battled to solve his citizenship status, inspiring the 2004 Steven Spielberg movie, *The Terminal*, staring Tom Hanks and Catherina Zeta-Jones. Unfortunately, Nasseri never got an on-screen smooch with Zeta-Jones, but he did receive a generous $300,000 from DreamWorks for the rights to his story. Ironically, he lacked a bank account to cash the check. Some guys just can't catch a break.

UGH! WHY THE F#%@ CAN'T I CHANGE MY TICKET?: AIRLINE CODES AND FARE CLASSES EXPLAINED

Have you ever run into the bathroom crying or thrown your phone out the window in complete exasperation after spending hours arguing with a ticket agent who explains that you can't change your ticket because you are flying on an *H*-class fare and any changes require upgrading to a full fare, which, unfortunately, will cost you a trillion dollars more? "Why do there have to be so many damn rules?" you may ask. The answer is fairly simple. You are not a movie star.

Until your Hollywood blockbuster grosses $100 million in its first week, or you become the next American Idol, you're going to have to play by the rules. And when it comes to the airline industry, the rules are endless.

In your quest for sanity, it may help for you to understand that all airfares are sold according to class, and then broken down into subclasses. Generally speaking, *F* and *P* refer to first class, *C* and *J* refer to business class, *Y* refers to full-fare coach, and *M*, *B*, *H*, *K*, *Q*, *L*, *V*, etc. refer to discounted coach fares. Each fare class has a specific list of rules detailing what can and can't be changed once the ticket is purchased.

For example, a reservation with a *Y* fare may be fully refundable or eligible for a free upgrade to first class, while an *M* fare booked on the same flight may be entitled to nothing more than a free bag of peanuts. These classes are standard across the industry, which is what enables ticket agents to quickly view the seat inventory of other airlines when they need to move passengers to another flight.

Additionally, every ticket purchased is assigned a fare basis code, such as ML14LNR. In this case, *M* refers to the fare class, *L* is for low season, 14 stands for 14-day advanced purchase, *L* for long-haul, and

NR for non-refundable. This little cryptogram is the airline's way of keeping track of just how much they can screw you when you try to change your ticket.

While all this may seem unduly complicated (and yes, unfair), remember a large majority of an airline's revenue comes from first-class and business-class seats sold at a premium. When fares in these classes sometimes run upward of $20,000, it stands to reason that an airline just may be inclined to take care of those passengers' needs before they rush to accommodate your two-for-one $49 Internet special.

Don't Sweat the Small Stuff—Wait for the Big One[17*]

The key to maintaining your sanity when flying is to not let the small stuff get in the way of enjoying your trip. This is no one's responsibility but your own. Sometimes you will get a phenomenal deal on a plane ticket and be treated with courtesy and respect everywhere you turn, and life will be just grand. Some days you'll wish to God you never got out of bed and that everyone you know lived in the same state so you never have to sep foot on a plane again. That's just life. Maintain your cool, and you'll be amazed at how much better things will be!

- If you are met with a particularly pigheaded or rude ticket agent on the phone, don't start crying (yet). Simply hang up and call back. If you get the same individual again, politely ask to be switched to a different person. If they come back on the line in a phony voice pretending to be someone else, use your own phony voice to tell them you were doing a random customer satisfaction survey, and they failed. (I would also book my ticket with another airline.)

- Instead of an "F--- You!" try a "Thank You!" Be overly thankful to everyone you encounter—it becomes addictive. If you forgot

---

17. That's good relationship advice too, passed on to me from my friend Ryan. Unfortunately, he neglected to provide me with an accurate method of recognizing the big one. I don't mind living in my car, but perhaps you might. Keep your eyes open out there kids!

to take your sword out of your carry-on and the security folks confiscate it, thank them for doing a good job. You can always buy another sword. If you get bumped, thank the ticket agent for helping you find a new flight. They could just as easily go on break and leave you stranded. In fact, thank everyone who goes out of their way to make your flying experience more enjoyable: Thank the pilot for making a nice landing. Thank the flight attendant for removing a blanket from a sleeping senior citizen and bringing it to you. Thank the person next to you for not drooling on your shoulder when she dozed off (unless you are a mother and are not bothered by drool). Thank people who write humorous travel books for your enjoyment. Thank your mom for giving birth to you.

Enough of this nice stuff—you get the idea. It's time to get back to business. We've got some serious time to kill here, so let's move on to the next chapter, my favorite!

Tying It All Together:
Christmas Miracles Can Happen

Several years ago my flight home for Christmas was cancelled for absolutely no reason, and I was told there were no available flights until December 27. The weather wasn't bad. The airline gave no explanation and no apology—nothing. If you've ever been in this situation, you can understand the devastation this can cause. I did everything right. I booked my ticket months in advance. I hadn't seen my family in nearly a year. I was understandably pissed. (Not to mention quite concerned Santa would give my presents to someone else if I wasn't there to collect them.) But something told me to remain calm.

Instead of yelling and screaming after being repeatedly informed there was nothing anyone could do, I kept calling the airline until I got through to an angel of a ticket agent who stayed on the phone with me for an hour and twenty minutes, until she finally received approval to rebook my coach ticket on a first-class seat on a nonstop red-eye flight with another airline. (Generally, that's not something that happens.) I arrived home just in time to see the sun rising on a sleepy, snow-covered Christmas morning.

I wish I knew that ticket agent's name so I could thank her. Hopefully, she'll read this and know that her efforts meant the world to me. As it turned out, that was the last Christmas I ever got to spend with my grandfather before he passed away. Sometimes, just being polite pays off in ways you might never expect.

CHAPTER 4

NOW WHAT THE HELL DO I DO?

You ever fly standby? It never works. That's why they call it standby.
You end up standing there going, 'Bye.   —Jerry Seinfeld

Now what? Ah, the age-old philosophical conundrum so many have pondered, yet so few have answered. What do I do now that football season is over? What do I do now that I graduated from college with an English degree? Or more simply, what the hell do I do now for the next few hours in airport hell?

Chances are, even if you're fortunate enough to not be delayed, you're going to find yourself having to kill a lot of time in the airport, caught up in an endless swarm of passengers while grudgingly taking part in the world's largest game of musical chairs.[18] Even if you are one of the lucky few to find a seat or some flat surface on which to rest your body, finding something to do is another thing entirely.

In the '70s and '80s, betting on flight-arrival times was a surefire way to kill some terminal time. But now with iPhones, BlackBerrys, and mobile devices delivering up-to-the-minute information at lightning speed, it's impossible to ensure a fair game. Equally outdated are games like solitaire, checkers, go fish, and thumb wrestling.

---

18. There is really no game of musical chairs. Please don't knock people to the ground should the music in the terminal suddenly turn off.

After nearly two decades of extensive, gut-wrenching, painstaking research, I have developed a wide variety of time wasters, updated for our modern, fast-paced digital age. Try one. Try them all. Some of these you can do by yourself. Others, you will need a willing partner. All of these activities will kill at least a minute or two and bring you one step closer to your elusive dream: getting on your flight.

AIRPORT TIME WASTERS

Level I (for the Productive, Practical Type)

- Review your portfolio allocations. If you don't have any portfolio allocations and keep all your money in checking, now might be an excellent time to buy a book on investing.

- Use this time to back up your laptop hard drive. Make a habit of doing this every time you fly, and you'll never have to worry about losing all your dirty pictures, er, I mean data, ever again.

- Scroll through your contacts and delete people you no longer like from your phone. You'll be surprised how good this can feel.

- Spend some time writing fake text messages to practice the fastest way to enter words using the text-ahead feature on your cell phone.

- Go through your phone and see how many times you sent a one-line text with the words OK or THNX or a smiley face and nothing else as a reply to a message, then review a recent copy of your cell phone bill. Compute how many thousands of dollars you could've saved by avoiding this. Then text your friends and tell them about it. LOL.

- Get your shoes shined. This is an aging tradition we need to bring back. These poor guys are always bored.

- Ladies, now would be an excellent time to clean out that mobile filing cabinet you refer to as a purse. Gentlemen, let's get the receipts and expired condoms out of those wallets.

- Call your mom.

Level II (for the Creative Type)

- Ask to borrow a confiscated pirate sword from the security bin so you can work on your parry and thrust, and your swashbuckling accent. (Make sure to return it before you get on board to avoid being taken down by a Federal Air Marshal.)

- Have someone untie your shoes and see how long it takes to get those knots back together using only one hand. Don't laugh. It's far harder than it looks.

- Challenge a third-grader sitting next to you and see who can name more state capitals. If she beats you, try naming countries that start with S. If she beats you again, try a push-up competition. If you've managed to encounter the next Hermione overachieving child sorcerer en route to Hogwarts School of Witchcraft and Wizardry, challenge her to a game of who's taller, and then go sit somewhere else. (And keep a watchful eye out so you don't get turned into a frog.)

Level III (for the Athletic Type)

Terminal B Obstacle Course

Gather up all the trash barrels in the terminal, and borrow some suitcases from fellow passengers and lay them out across the floor in a makeshift obstacle course. Invite a high school sports team to compete against you (there's always one traveling somewhere, easily recognizable by their matching polyester warm-up suits), and have someone record your times. See if you can get the ticket agents to post your best time up on the Arrivals/Departures board.

Set a New World Record

What better place for a world record attempt than a terminal full of verifiable witnesses with nothing better to do than watch you become part of history? And unless your layover is in some alternate universe, it's guaranteed at least one person will have a video camera on them to capture your glorious achievement. Below are some current world records that can be attempted without any additional preparation or equipment. (Just keep in mind, whatever record you set, Michael Phelps will eventually beat you.)

- Most nonstop push-ups: 10,507, by Minoru Yoshida, Japan, 1980.

- Most push-ups in one hour: 5,000 by Manjunath S. Devadiga of Bhatkal (it's near Pakistan), 2007.

- Longest time spent in full-body contact with ice: 1 hour and 30 minutes by Wang Jintu, Beijing, 2008. (You may have a tough time getting the ice past security. Have some friends help you grab some from the soda fountains in the terminal.)

- Most sit-ups in one minute: 196, by Patrick Broe, United Kingdom, 2008.

- Fastest time for pushing an orange one mile with your nose: 24 minutes, 36 seconds, by Ashrita Furman, actually recorded at JFK Airport, New York, 2005.

- Most T-shirts worn at once: 224, by Charlie Williams, United Kingdom, 2008. (Charlie also wins a *Please Hug Me* Award of Excellence for the Most Ingenious Way to Avoid Paying the $25 extra-baggage fee.)

- Longest handstand: For some reason, information on this particular record is unavailable. Perhaps the folks at Guinness are trying to discourage any further attempts after too many people have died from blood rushing to their head. But I did discover that Andy R. holds the longest handstand record at Consul Elementary School in Saskatchewan, Canada, with a rather unspectacular 3.75 seconds (after his third try).

HOW ATTRACTIVE AM I REALLY?

This is a pretty simple game that requires little preparation and little set-up time, although it's not for the faint of heart. Results can have lasting psychological damage.

It's a known fact that we love it when pretty people smile at us. Pretty-people smiles make us feel warm inside and remind us that even though we've lost some hair or our breasts have sunk to the ground after bringing three children into the world (probably should've gotten little Timmy on solid food a little sooner), at least someone out there still finds us attractive. Of course, when we receive that very same smile from an ugly person, it creeps us out for the rest of the day.

To determine where you rank on the pretty versus hideous scale (and kill a little time), approach one hundred random people in the terminal and offer them your best I'm-being-friendly-but-not-in-a-gay-way smile.

Steps for a Proper I'm-Being-Friendly-but-Not-in-a-Gay-Way Smile

1. Catch the gaze of someone within ten to fifteen feet of you.
2. Pause for a moment, then soften your eyes.

3. Purse your lips and raise the corners of your mouth to a height equal to or less than one-third the width of your mouth. Be sure not to show any teeth. People will mistake this for craziness. Practice this technique by tucking a dime into the corner of your mouth where your lips meet your cheek. If the dime falls out, you are smiling too hard. (For those of you with unusually large mouths, you can use a quarter.)

4. A slight eyebrow raise wouldn't be entirely inappropriate.

Now, for each person who smiles back, award yourself two points. Subtract one point for anyone who is repulsed by your advances. Award yourself an extra five points if you were stuck in the terminal all night and didn't shower but still pulled some major smileage. Below is a score sheet for accurate tallying. (I've gone ahead and given you a few points as a little confidence boost. I know you are one good-looking human.)

Note: if you have a mustache, you may want to shave it for this game, as it might make it difficult to notice your charming smile.

How Attractive Am I Really Score Sheet

Smiled Back Warmly* (2 points)	Acknowledged Politely (1 point)	No Noticeable Change (–1 point)	Turned and Ran (–5 points)	Blind (N/A)
⧸⧸⧸⧸⧸				
TOTALS:				

*You can assume a variance of +/– 5 percent for other people reading this book and playing the same game. Sorry, their smiles don't count.

Score: 90–100 = You're a major hottie.

80–89 = You're one sexy babe.

70–79 = You're lookin' fine.

60–69 = You won't get kicked out of bed.

50–59 = After one or two beers, they'll love you.

40–49 = Maybe you should dig that gym membership gift cer-
tificate out of the trash.

30–39 = Remember that new hairstyle you've been thinking
about . . . go for it!

20–29 = It's not your fault the world is based on looks.

10–19 = You do have other skills, right?

00–10 = I'm sorry.

You can play this game anywhere you like, but a crowded airport terminal is a perfect location given the random population sampling you will encounter. If you are really low on self-esteem and wish to skew the odds in your favor, consider booking a flight through Miami, Orlando, San Diego, or any happy, warm vacation destination where smiles run aplenty. Be sure to avoid any airport within a fifty-mile radius of New York City (or Canada) in the winter.

CELEBRITY "SIGHTING"

Celebrity "Sighting" works best in some of the smaller airports around the country. Pick a random person sitting next to you and ask them if they're local to the area, and if they see a lot of movie stars in these parts. They'll probably admit that no, they rarely see movie stars here, and go back to reading their James Patterson mystery or munching on their fajita burrito wrap. As soon as you're sure they're not look-ing, point to the back of someone who just walked by and say, "Hey, isn't that the guy who played the neighbor on *Married With Children*?" (David Garrison). They'll likely make some remark like, "Huh. Well, I'll be damned," and go back to their Patterson/fajita.

Wait a few minutes, then make another celebrity "sighting," this time moving slightly up the celebrity ladder. "Whoa. I think that was Fran Drescher?!" (The huge-bosomed nanny with the tiny waist and the crazy laugh.) Remark how strange it was to see two celebrities like that in a row, then gauge the local's reaction. If he begins to show some signs of interest, start pushing the envelope. See how far you can get before you have to board your plane.

It will help if you familiarize yourself with the back of as many celebrity heads as possible. Just pick up a copy of *US* magazine and flip to the page with the photographs of celebrities making out.

Celebrity "Sighting" Rankings

Beginner: Examples of Sub-B Level Celebs

Girl from Tostitos Super Bowl commercials, Webster, Kirk Cameron from Growing Pains, Bakithi Kumalo (Paul Simon's bass player), any ensign from Star Trek who appeared in one episode and was killed off after being picked to visit a mysterious planet

Intermediate: Examples of B-Level Celebs

Steve Buscemi, Stephen Hawking, Al Franken, Mandy Patinkin, Sarah Michelle Gellar,[19] any member of R.E.M., Weird Al Yankovic

Expert: Examples of A-Level Celebs

Tom Cruise, Jim Carey, Michael Jordan, Jennifer Aniston, Stephen Colbert[20]

Advanced: Examples of World-Renowned Figures

Pamela Anderson, Prince Charles, the artist formerly/currently known as Prince, the president of the United States, or the pope. (Go with John

---

19.   Sorry SMG. We're still anxiously waiting for *Buffy the Vampire Slayer: The Next Generation* before we're awarding you A-level status again. The *I Know What You Did Last Summer* sequels aren't cutting it. (They brought *90210* back. Anything is possible.) And the no-nudity clause in your contract isn't helping matters either. I bought every calendar you've ever graced the cover of, and rarely do I need to know what day it is. The least you could do is show us some of the goods.
20.   According to him.

Paul II even though he's dead 'cause no one knows the new dude, and he's already looking like he might not make it that long anyway.) And yes, they all start with a P here in the advanced level.

This is also an excellent way to meet middle-aged women at the airport bar. What mother of three wouldn't be flattered to be mistaken for Valerie Bertinelli or Sally Field? I'd advise against approaching younger women as they generally don't take too kindly to pickup lines involving, "Hey darling, you know who you look like . . . ?" (Because all young women think they are movie stars.)

Worthy of note: Don't bother playing Celebrity "Sighting" in Salt Lake City International Airport, unless you are very familiar with Mormon TV stars. If you insist, check out Famousmormons.net, where competition for the A-list includes Wilford Brimley, Brady Bluhm (the voice of Christopher Robin in *Winnie the Pooh*), and Eliza Dushku, who also reigns supreme on the list of Famous Mormon Vampires for her role on *Buffy the Vampire Slayer*. (Careful. There are more Mormon Vampires out there than you might think.)

BATHROOM BINGO

For a while now, I've been a big believer of the theory that we humans are getting too far ahead of ourselves on the technology curve, and have invented far too many things we don't need. (See "SkyMall Shopping" in chapter 6.) Nowhere is this more apparent than in the airport restroom.

What happened to the water and paper towel system that had been working fine for the last hundred years? Can you recall a time a decade ago when you left a bathroom complaining about your clean, properly sanitized, adequately dry hands? Doubtful. But now we have faucets so technologically advanced, they already know when your hands are clean and refuse to dispense even one more drop of water than necessary. These pompous, tree-hugging faucets are so hell-bent on conserving our precious resources and saving the environment one dirty hand at a time that they refuse to accept their position in the man-versus-machine hierarchy. At least I have come to assume that this is why I can never get them to work, and as a result, have to continually purchase $5 Homeland Security Bottled Water to rinse the pink lotion-soap off my hands.[21]

To my knowledge, I have standard-size wrists, and my depth perception is fairly accurate. Also, I'm not an idiot, although I've resembled one more times than I care to admit while waving my arms like a drunken marionette in front of the bathroom mirror, trying to locate the hidden sensor and draw a single drop of water from these stingy, metallic demons. (I've also struggled with the automatic toilets from time to time, but I've never been quite as concerned about them. Standing up and sitting down is a good workout for the quads, and well, let's face it. If it doesn't flush, it ain't my problem.)

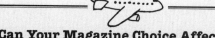

Can Your Magazine Choice Affect Your Chance at Dry Hands?

It's called the Xcelerator. It's the latest and greatest in airport bathroom hand-drying technology. It can dry your hands in fewer than ten seconds and allegedly saves thousands of trees a year. It will also rip the upper epidermis off your skin, blow your hairpiece off your head, and blast the buttons off your blouse

---

21. The soap dispensers always work. Perfect irony, or government conspiracy? You be the judge.

should you inadvertently step in front of this shiny-steeled menace. (Granted, a few missing buttons may help you get through security faster, but they will also earn you a substantial amount of cell phone pics posted on the Internet. Tough call.)

Though it is cleverly marketed as an ecological marvel, you and I are both smart enough to know this modern miracle has a hidden agenda: taking over the planet.

Yes my fellow travelers, I hate to be the one to inform you, but machines are taking over, beginning with our airport restrooms.[22] Because if we can't poop in peace, what do we have really?

The Xcelerator must be stopped.

Now, don't get me wrong. I like trees as much as the next person. Probably more, considering the amount of time I spend in hammocks eating maple syrup. But a tree should not be denied its innate right to be turned into a paper towel because some of you can't control yourselves around McDonald's napkins and refuse to recycle. It's because of people like you that the Xcelerator is threatening our way of life. Oh, and the Dyson Airblade digital motor inverted hand dryer? Don't get me started. (I dare you to slide your hands inside that 400 mph jet stream and tell me you don't feel as though you're being violated.)

Is there a solution, then, to this vital ecological conundrum? Some way that we can dry our hands peacefully while protecting the integrity of the rainforests? Yes. Quit printing

---

22. Don't believe me? Wait and see. First, it's our inability to control the dryness of our own hands. Then it's automatic coffeemakers that brew coffee before we even wake up, forcing caffeine on us and systematically wearing down our nervous systems. What's next? Talking boxes in our living rooms, broadcasting moving images depicting real people living together and competing in unusual challenges, with hypnotic soundtracks and highly addictive editing that makes it impossible to turn away while these talking boxes proceed to suck the life force from our very beings? Listen up machines! We will not go down without a fight! What's that? Oh, Big Brother XXXIV is back on? Never mind.

bibles. (Kidding. Kidding. How else would we get anyone to tell the truth in court?)

The real solution? Health and Fitness Magazine Consolidation.

Next time you're in the airport bookstore, suck in your gut, put down your venti frappuccino for a moment, and take a look at the news rack. Count how many magazines say exactly the same thing. Actually, I've already done the work for you. The answer is 127. There are 127 health magazines published each month telling you what you already know: You're lazy.

There are no new "breakthrough" routines, ab crunches, sweat-'til-you-die power yoga moves, or amazing fat-burning secrets that will tighten your Big Mac buns. In fact, human beings have known the secret to healthy living for more than two thousand years: run more, eat less. (Have you seen the abs on those apostles? Jesus would be hard pressed to pull that miracle trick and feed the masses today. "Dammit Judas! I said take *one* piece of bread and pass it down. I swear. You're gonna be the death of me.")

So let's take a stand. Let's take all these publications and combine them into one mega magazine called "Lazy American." We'll publish it biannually and use the millions of trees we're saving to get some hardcore, heavy-duty, two-ply, hypoallergenic, real-man paper towels back in these bathrooms. Your hands will be happy, dry, and ready to love you again.

Come to think of it, we should probably do the same thing with the golf magazines. There are no new tips about behind-the-back bunker shots or impossible fairway lies that are going to improve your score, as golf is simply impossible.

And while we're at it, everyone needs to stop writing checks and insisting on paper bank statements.[23] Have you ever heard a tree cry? It's sad.

There was actually no game here. I just wanted to see if anyone else out there has the same hand-washing problems I do, but I knew you would skip over this section if there were no promise of fun. I–29. Bingo!

HUG ME GAMES OF SKILL

Game of Skill 1: Home Sweet Homeland

This game is fairly simple. Pretend to be part of Homeland Security. Randomly go up to people and inform them they've been selected for additional screening. Be polite, but firm. Insist they come with you. Award one point for every person who actually considers following you. Two points for anyone who stands up and tells their family not to wait for them if they don't return. Five points for anyone who allows you to lead them into a restroom and drops their pants for a cavity search.

Game of Skill 2: Starbucks Surprise

Within each terminal lies a Starbucks. And within each Starbucks lies a bored Starbucks employee. "How can anyone be bored when they are

---

23.   Okay, this is actually just directed at my parents, who don't necessarily fear the Internet, but who think it's not quite for them. Their unintentional use of trees that could've been made into paper towels could be saving their son the embarrassment of having to wipe his hands on his jeans, resulting in giant wet spots, and thus effectively prohibiting a chance meeting with any potential soul mate and pushing the shot at grandchildren even further into the future. Sorry, Mom. You're doing this to yourself.

surrounded by so much whipped cream?" you may ask. Because airport Starbucks have no local customer base with names to learn and favorite drinks to memorize—one of the vocational joys for the aspiring Starbucks employee.

To kill a little time while helping these fine folks fully live out their barista dreams, order some sort of coffee and steamed milk concoction and be sure to tell the person at the register your name as you pass through the line. They may act like they don't care, but they do. (Careful. Some may recognize you as the guy who uses their green apron to get through security.) Proceed to drink your coffee as quickly as you can, then return to the line and order another. They'll be happy to see you so soon. "Okay, so that's a tall mocha frappuccino with six shots of boysenberry for . . . hey, it's Jim, right?" "Right," you'll say. (Unless your name is not "Jim," in which case politely correct them—or just roll with it.) Pay for your frappuccino and down this second one as fast as possible. Return to the line and repeat the procedure until your flight departs, or until your nervous system shuts down from caffeine overdose.

The next time you travel through that particular airport, you can take pride in knowing you'll be the one and only customer who took the time to care. Be sure to look for the little plaque with your name up there as the very first Customer of the Month in the history of the Terminal B Starbucks. Great work, Jim!

Game of Skill 3: 99 Degrees

I can't take credit for this one since it was invented by my good friend and guitarist extraordinaire, Scott Barkan. It's a modern twist on Twenty Questions, devised while touring on the road. But it can certainly be adapted for airport layovers.

It takes two to play this game, and the rules are quite simple. Person one (let's call him Jeff) picks something in the universe, and person two (let's call him Scott) has to guess what it is in five questions or fewer. The only clue you are allowed to give the other person is a degree percentage of how close his guess is.

For example, if the thing in the universe Jeff picked was a car, and Scott's first guess is a computer, Jeff would award Scott 40 percent for choosing an inanimate object beginning with the same letter. But if the tables were turned, Scott might award Jeff only 5 percent, based on the fact that a car's primary purpose is transportation, while a computer's is for porn.

The beauty is, you don't have to explain to your opponent your rationale, just the percentage. Impossible you say? Don't be so sure. If you can believe it, this game has actually been won on the very first guess. Although to be fair, the item chosen was fairly obvious: Rick Astley, "Never Gonna Give You Up" CD single, circa 1988. Well, duh.

Hug Me Bonus: I'll Be Home for Christmas . . . if Only in My Dreams

Everyone dreads traveling around the holidays. There's white powder everywhere, excruciating delays, angry customers . . . and that's just the line at the Dunkin' Donuts inside the airport.[24]

But, we still do it—every single year.

Understand that the holiday season is the busiest time of year for airlines, as it is for every other industry that relies on Jesus to resurrect their dismal yearly sales. And here in North America, the busiest travel season coincides nicely with the most unpredictable weather season, making for all kinds of wet, wintry fun. Just a few inches of snow can cause delays and cancel flights across the country, leaving thousands of angry passengers who need to be rerouted, and who grow angrier by

---

24. I'm well aware that this one requires the snare-and-cymbal hit from a late-night talk show band to effectively sell the joke. I'll be sure to include the appropriate sound effect on the audio book version, but if you could just do it out loud while you're reading along, that would be really helpful. Ba dum bum.

the moment as they wait in line and watch as thousands of other passengers are rerouted before them.

Can you do anything about it? No. In fact, if you recycle, bought a Prius, or voted for Al Gore, you are only contributing to the problem. (Mother Earth hates snow just as much as I do and has been trying her best to warm this place up. But no, you have to go and buy those foolish energy-efficient lightbulbs to try and keep global warming in check—shame on you.) This means that if you are flying anywhere in the month of December, chances are very high that your flight is going to be delayed and your bags may end up in Alaska.[25] So just accept it.

During the holidays airline employees are pushed to their absolute capacity, often working fourteen- or sixteen-hour shifts. Do not take your frustrations out on them. They are doing the best they can. Unless they're not doing the best they can, in which case still don't yell. Just pull out a nine iron and take a couple of casual practice swings while you stand at the counter, then ask them, "So, hypothetically, let's say you were Tiger Woods. Would you be able to get me on a flight out of here any sooner?" (If they still answer no, well, then you're screwed. If TW can't do it, it can't be done.)

In the meantime, have a little fun. Tape jingle bells to your kids and make them dance for everyone in the terminal. Pack an iPod full of holiday tunes and keep your headphones on 24/7. Spend a little extra time at the airport bar. After all, the holidays were meant for catching up with old friends, like Jack Daniels and Jim Beam. Do whatever it takes to get into the holiday spirit.

More Holiday Travel Survival Tips

■ Book your holiday travel as early as you can. Prices are not going down. Really, they're not.

---

25. Assuming here most readers wouldn't be flying to Alaska for the holidays. If you are, kindly substitute another faraway state where your bags are going to likely end up.

■ If you find yourself stuck in an insanely long line at the ticket counter and are worried about missing your flight, put on a Santa hat, dress up your wife and kids in reindeer antler headbands, and wait patiently in line. There's no guarantee a ticket agent will believe you are truly Santa Claus and bump you to the front, but there's no guarantee they won't. No one wants to be responsible for causing Christmas to be cancelled.

■ Remember, everything you carry on board has to go through security, and taking a ton of presents with you just lengthens the lines for everyone and makes the TSA agent's job that much harder. Only bring presents for those family members you actually like, or the ones that might leave you some money when they die. Chances are, this will lighten your load considerably.

■ Instead of carrying bulky gifts like turtleneck sweaters for your nieces and nephews, make a donation to a charity in their names. They won't speak to you again, but this will help prepare them for bitter disappointment later in life.

■ If you insist on bringing presents with you, never wrap them. Security can and will unwrap all your packages to make sure there is nothing dangerous inside, as well as making sure you're not trying to regift something you got from the office Christmas party.

■ Pack a toothbrush and a change of clothes in your carry-on. If your luggage gets lost you'll at least have clean teeth, and you won't have to borrow your father-in-law's argyle sweater for Christmas dinner.

■ A wonderful way to celebrate the season is to pick up a few copies of this book for the people you love. Fits easily into any carry-on and makes an excellent stocking stuffer, or a suitable gift for Days 1 through 7 of Chanukah. (You might want to splurge for something a little more expensive for Day 8.)

■ Are you still waiting to book that holiday season ticket? Seriously, what's wrong with you?

And eventually, yes, even during the holidays you will find yourself finally able to board your plane. Here's where the real fun begins. Because here is where you're going to have to confront your greatest fear—and I'm not talking about turbulence, or being the lone New York Yankee fan on a flight heading to Boston.

I'm talking about something far worse.

Turn the page, if you dare.

CHAPTER 5

IN THE AIR ... FINALLY?

Take my money, take my wife ... just don't take my cell phone

Psst. Hey there. Yes, you. I bet you're feeling a bit lonely right now.

In fact, I bet after putting all your clothes back on after passing through the metal detectors and purchasing your $12 tuna sandwich and $5 bottle of Homeland Security Super Water, you suddenly feel more alone than at any other time in your life. Why? Because even though you may be riding the high of conquering some Level III Airport Time Wasters and beating the entire Washington Valley High basketball team at your Terminal B obstacle course, you know what lies ahead.

Deep down you know that as soon as you pass through that little tunnel and take your seat on board the plane, you are going to come face-to-face with your greatest fear. Deep down you know that when you hear the rumble of the engines firing up, and you feel the plane backing away from the gate, the flight attendant is going to come on with her little announcement, pleasantly reminding you that federal law prohibits the use of cell phones and any electronic communication device for the duration of your flight.

That's silly, you might say. I don't need my cell phone to make me feel secure. I can hop aboard a plane and go as long as I need without my phone.

Really? Can you?

Are you aware the fastest-growing neurological disorder in the world today is a condition that affects more lives than AIDS, heart disease, genital herpes, and the bird flu combined?

It's a condition knows as PVS, or phantom vibration syndrome, and according to the Center for Disease Control in Atlanta, Georgia, there is no known cure.

PVS occurs when people claim to feel a vibration in their hip pocket, or wherever they normally carry their cell phone or BlackBerry, only to find that there is no call or message when they check the device. Some sufferers report feeling upward of a hundred vibrations a day, often when they're not even carrying their phone. Extreme cases have been reported of individuals waking up in the middle of the night in a cold sweat, scrambling to answer nonexistent calls and imaginary texts, while sympathetic spouses pat their foreheads with a warm washcloth and try to calm their fears.

Google it. It's real. And it's deadly.

Doctors have compared PVS sensations to those experienced by amputees who have lost a limb in a war, or in a good bar fight. *A limb.* This is how dependent society has become on personal communication devices. And it's only getting worse.

The average adult checks his or her cell phone approximately 7,189 times a day. That's approximately once every twelve seconds. And now, here you are, standing in front of the gate, facing the next several hours of complete and utter communication blackout. You could be going ten times as long as the radio silence when Armstrong and the boys went around to the dark side of the moon.

No phone. No e-mail. No BlackBerry. No texting. No instant messenger. No string tied to a can. No communication with the outside world at all. Your only chance for human contact limited to the other hundred or so passengers crammed with you inside a tiny metal tube hurtling through the atmosphere.

The whole lot of you are trusting your lives to strangers who care about you so much that they lock themselves behind an impenetrable door for the duration of your flight. Strangers you just assume are experienced (and sober) enough to transport you safely to your destination, no matter what lies ahead: hurricanes, tornadoes, alien spacecraft, or worst of all, an in-flight movie staring Keanu Reeves. Anything could

Fanny Pack for Your Seat

Have trouble deciding what you need with you in your seat? Hate getting up and down to pull stuff from your bag in the overhead bin because you know everyone seated near you is checking out your bottom? Check out the Nirvana Seatback Organizer from Zen Class. Their handy organizer hooks on the back of your tray table and comes with specially designed pockets to hold your tickets, passport, cell phone, magazines, iPod, DVD player, earphones, and pretty much anything else you might carry on board (including this book). The ultimate gift for the person in your life with OCD.

You can also take comfort in knowing that in the event of a water landing, while everyone else is scrambling for the exits and abandoning everything they own in the overhead compartments, you'll be only one zipper away from surviving life on a deserted island in comfort. Grab your water-resistant Seatback Organizer, jump down the slide, then pull out your iPod as you await rescue. Now that's Nirvana. Visit Zenclasstravel.com.

happen. And you won't be able tell a soul about it other than the person sitting next to you.

You can feel your palms beginning to sweat, and your hands starting to tremble as you reach for the power button on your phone. How can you possibly handle this?

TIPS FOR OVERCOMING CELL PHONE SEPARATION ANXIETY

Oh ye of little faith. I would never present a problem without a solution for you. (It's called earning your reader's trust.) As a fellow sufferer of phantom vibration syndrome, I hereby testify that I have learned to adjust, and now I actually welcome a few hours of isolation and freedom from my vibrating pocket. It's been challenging, but I've survived. And you can too! Here's how:

- If this is your first flight, ask a flight attendant to reseat you as close to the front of the plane as possible. If they can seat you inside the little closet right behind the cockpit, even better. With fewer people in front of you, there will be less excitement for you to watch, and fewer things you'll have the urge to call and tell someone about. If you're stuck in the back of the plane, try to focus on the clouds.

- Buy a toy cell phone and take it on board with you. If you feel the uncontrollable urge to make a call, pull it out and dial whatever preprogrammed numbers come with the phone. You may end up talking to Barbie, Ken, Scooby-Doo, Grimace, or any variety of characters from Sesame Street, but they'll be glad you called.

- When something pops into your head and you feel the itch to call your friends and tell them about it, take out a piece of paper and write it down. This will get it off your mind, and help you relax knowing you won't forget to tell them later. (Actually, this is a good idea in general. When you reread what you wrote you'll realize just how amazing it is you even have any friends.) And, of course, when you land you can call your girlfriends and tell them how you wrote down everything you were going to tell them and then you realized it really wasn't that important after all, and oh my God, you should've seen the hottie pilot that just walked by, and oh, you're never gonna believe this, but did you know that Scooby-Doo actually sounds just like Astro from *The Jetsons* when you call him on the phone, and . . . hello? Sarah? Hello?

FIRST CLASS BLONDES AND BULKHEAD BEAUTIES

A man finds a blonde sitting in his seat in first class. He says, "Excuse me miss, but I believe this is my seat." She replies, "I'm blonde, I'm beautiful, I have a great body, and I'm going to New York." So the guy calls the flight attendant over to help him.

He explains the situation to the flight attendant, and the flight attendant says, "Miss, your seat is in coach, I'm gonna have to ask you to leave first class." The blonde responds, "I'm blonde, I'm beautiful, I have a great body, and I'm going to New York."

The flight attendant then goes to get the captain to help, and the captain asks the blonde to please leave first class and go back to coach. The blonde responds, "I'm blonde, I'm beautiful, I have a great body, and I'm going to New York." The captain pauses for a minute, then whispers something in the blonde's ear. Immediately, she gets up and goes back to coach.

The flight attendant is amazed, and asks the captain, "What did you say to get her to move?"

The captain replies, "I told her first class doesn't go to New York."

Ah, yes, an oldie but goodie. Almost as offensive to blondes as it is to anyone who doesn't realize the guy in the joke just blew his chances with a beautiful, hot-bodied woman. But it does illustrate the point that yes, even the stereotypical less-than-intelligent blonde understands the best way to travel is in first class. Unfortunately, no matter how hard most of us work, traveling in the lap of luxury every time we fly is simply not in the cards. Until our proverbial ships come in (or the real ones if you've lost so much money in the stock market you've been forced to join a Somali pirate crew to rebuild your 401(k)), we're going to have to wage our battles in coach. At least there is one beauty back there to share our misery.

If you are going to remain with your fellow commoners behind the cotton curtain, the best you can do is book a seat in Section BB, home to the Bulkhead Beauties. These are the seats located directly behind the partitions that separate the cabin into different sections, commonly referred to as bulkheads. These are by far the best coach seats on any plane for a number of reasons:

- With no one in front of you, you can put your feet up on the wall and pretend you're the president aboard Air Force One in your own private office.

- You have extra room in front of you to stand up, stretch, do push-ups, receive a lap dance from a flight attendant, etc.

- Your tray tables come out of the armrests. You can arm wrestle your neighbor, practice your drum solos for Rock Band, or throw a tantrum if they run out of peanuts by the time they get to your row. Pound away on your tray the entire flight without worrying about annoying the person in front of you.

- Your personal TV is also located in the armrest. Not really a bene-fit, but it does make you feel like you're on board a cool spaceship.

- If they are filming a movie or a TV commercial on your flight, this is where they will set up the camera and the crew. It could be a nice opportunity to learn about the art of cinematography.

The only disadvantage to sitting in these seats, is there is no underseat storage for a carry-on. Feel free to toss your bag in the flight attendant closet. I'm sure they won't mind. Also note, if you ask a ticket agent to sit you in Section BB, you'll probably get a funny look. (It's not real.)

Bulkhead Booking Tip

Many airlines only allow exit row seats or bulkhead seats to be booked the day of a flight. Check in online as soon as your flight becomes available, which is generally twenty-four hours prior to your departure time, then see if you can swap your cramped middle seat for a nice comfy exit row.

THE CHRONIC SEAT KICKER

I know that none of you reading this book have ever repeatedly kicked the seat in front of you during a flight. Or dug through the little seat-back compartment like Jack Cousteau searching for hidden treasure on the bottom of the Atlantic. Or shuffled a deck of cards on the tray table the *entire* length of a cross-country trip (I knew that kid behind me was gonna be trouble the moment I sat down). Or committed any of the other assortment of licentious, indecorous, dissolute activities that involve disrupting the comfort of the person sitting immediately in front of you. (Amazing how many words you can find in the English language to describe things people do that piss you off.)

In fact, I know all of you are amazing human beings. But there exists a legion of chronic seat kickers (CSKs), all part of the Me Generation, out in full force, and, miraculously, seated right behind you on yet another flight. One would think that even those suffering from severe depth perception would eventually realize their tray tables are connected to the person in front of them. Yet somehow, this information fails to register in their feeble minds, leaving us to spend an entire flight wallowing in the misery of some very unnecessary private turbulence.

Should I say something? Do I turn around and stare? Should I press my call button and have a Federal Air Marshal remove them from the plane? What if they have a malfunctioning prosthetic leg? I'll feel like a fool.

Yes, the risk of insulting someone with a prosthetic leg is something we all must deal with every day, but when you're facing five solid hours of air travel, you can't let that worry stop you from seeking your own comfort. It's best to deal with the problem before it gets out of hand. First it's your seat being kicked. Then your blanket goes missing. Next you find yourself wrapped in a cocoon of human gas, struggling for a breath of fresh air. Don't become a victim.

CSKs Ages Three Through Eleven

The first thing to realize about a young CSK is that as much as you want to blame them for acting out of control, it's not their fault. It's their parents' fault for raising them like a barbarian. But, left unchecked, the young CSK will continue to pelt the back of your seat relentlessly with youthful vigor and complete lack of concern for your sanity. Your first instinct may be to turn around and stare at them angrily, but that will have no effect. They will only recognize this as the look mommy gives them when she has to pick them up from daycare instead of spending the afternoon with the man who cleans the pool, or the look daddy gives them when they walk in on daddy while he's taking a nap with his secretary. They will continue to kick in defiance.

Instead, smile nicely, and ask them if they know the song about the leg bone connected to the knee bone, the knee bone connected to the thigh bone, etc. Ask them to sing along with you, then substitute the second verse with "the tray table's connected to my seatback, my seatback's connected to my backbone, my backbone's connected to me." You should begin to see the light dawn in their eyes. (Kids learn things much quicker when there is a melody associated with it.) Then break off a piece of your cookie and give it to them.

They'll be so shocked someone took the time to show them some affection, they'll remain a perfect angel for the rest of the trip. Don't be surprised if you find them trying to sneak into your suitcase, begging to come home with you.

CSKs Ages Twelve Through Seventeen

At this age a CSK is going through so many changes they may have no clue what's going on in the world around them. Their voices are dropping an octave a day and they are sprouting pubic hair faster than a Chia Pet. The teenager behind you may have walked on board at 5' 4", but after spending a few hours at thirty thousand feet with much less gravity pull, an in-flight growth spurt may find him deplaning at 6' 2". The sprouting teen can hardly be faulted for giving your seat the occasional boot. Or, what you may have mistaken for kicking could be the teenage girl behind you, struggling to keep her new breasts inside her training bra. Try to give them a little slack. High school is tough enough.

Adult CSKs

There is simply no excuse for an adult CSK. They deserve all the humiliation and punishment coming to them. The moment you find your backside pelted by an adult CSK, wait until the seatbelt signs are turned off, then stand up and announce that you have a small announcement to make.[26] After you are certain you have the entire cabin's attention, announce you'd like to offer to switch seats with anyone who prefers a seat that comes with personal massage vibration, then point directly at the CSK behind you. (Be careful not to move too quickly or wave your arms too wildly, or you may find yourself taken down by a Federal Air Marshal.)

Someone may actually offer to switch seats with you, in which case, problem solved. If not, just sit back down and enjoy the remainder of your flight in kick-free comfort. The CSK will likely mumble some apology about not realizing he was even kicking you, at which point you can now ask if it's because he has a prosthetic leg.

You may get some strange looks from the passengers around you, but what do you care? You're never going to see these people again. Except of course in the event of a water landing, which would likely require some time together on a deserted island. Best to learn to sleep with one eye open—you may be voted most likely to be eaten.

Senior Citizen CSKs

Try to have pity. Chances are elderly CSKs may have little control of their limbs. And remember, you might be there yourself one day. But if the geriatric assault on your comfort is still too much to handle, offer to play a game of Michigan Rummy with them. They'll be ecstatic.

---

26. I'm aware that announcing you have an announcement to make is redundant, but people get so into their little private TV screens on the plane it can take a while for them to look up. If you don't believe that to be true, look around you the next time a flight attendant is giving their little safety speech. It's amazing how many people would rather watch The Food Network than learn how to save their own lives. (That Giada is pretty adorable though.)

Afterward, they'll be so tired from the experience they'll just nod off peacefully for the rest of the flight. Just keep in mind, you can never actually beat a senior citizen at Michigan Rummy, so be sure not to wager on the game. And feel free to list this on your resume or college application as community service. It definitely counts.

Surviving a Flight Seated Next to a Lavatory

If you find yourself unfortunate enough to be seated next to a lavatory where people assume they can stand in front of you while waiting in line to do their thing, watching over your every move, and offering unwanted advice on your unfinished Sudoku, you may need to come out of your passive-aggressive shell for just a brief moment. You can avoid this by taping up a small sign that reads "Federal Regulations Prohibit You from Standing in Front of Me." People fear Federal Regulations.

SILENCE CRYING BABIES ONCE AND FOR ALL (1 GB IPOD REQUIRED)

Red-eye (n.): color of your eyes after an overnight flight seated near a crying baby

How many times have you hopped aboard a red-eye flight, settled into your seat, put on your little eye mask, and drifted off into a peaceful, gentle sleep, with that beautiful recurring dream playing in your head (you know, the one where your wife's cute girlfriend stays over and there's nowhere for her to sleep except your bed), only to be suddenly jolted awake by a baby's sharp cry, the single worst sound you could possibly imagine on an aircraft?

Why a parent with any sort of conscience would cause a plane full of passengers to suffer endlessly is beyond the scope of human comprehension. Any politician seeking office could easily win a campaign with a bill banning babies from red-eye flights. There is simply no need for a crying baby to be traveling after 10PM (9 Central).

If a crying baby is going to visit grandma, which is really the only place crying babies can be headed because they don't have any friends, they should just as easily be able to fly during the day. Grandparents are available to pick up crying babies from the airport 24/7. In fact, that's the only reason they are still alive. You will never hear a grandparent say, "Oh, we'd love to come get you dear, but you're coming in too late. Any chance you could hop the red-eye so we can pick you up after morning canasta?"

I'm sure at some point as you've waited to board a flight you've seen a mother breastfeeding her baby twins right in the middle of the terminal, and you tried to convince yourself not to sweat it—they won't be on your flight. Then, you watched in horror as the mother gathered up her offspring and duffle bags jam-packed with diapers and rattles then hopped to the front of the very line you'd been waiting in for preboarding. And, as sure as the sun will shine, as you step onto that plane and walk down the aisle, out of the hundreds of potential seats on the hundreds of commercial aircraft flying in and out of that airport, you manage to find the one seat right next to the little enemies.

According to the FAA, a captain of an aircraft has the right to refuse permission to board to anyone he feels poses a threat to the security of his vessel. If you can convince the captain that a baby is a national security threat, you may be in luck. Unfortunately, most babies are aware of this, and they are trained to not make a sound until an airplane reaches thirty thousand feet—or until you fall asleep.

As with most noble adversaries, the only way to beat the enemy is to think like the enemy. Hopefully you remembered to toss your iPod in your carry-on. It's go time soldier.

Crying Baby Playlist 1: Ages One Through Two

The only reason a baby cries at this age is because he wants little more than to crawl back into the womb from which he came. Babies want milk and the occasional raspberry blown on their bellies. That's it. They have little desire to be streaking through the nighttime sky at five hundred miles per hour, with thirty thousand feet of cabin pressure bearing down on their little baby ears. Yelling at them or waving a rattle in front of their faces will do little to silence their wailings.

If a baby is crying, ask their inconsiderate parents if it would be okay to put your headphones on them for a bit. Explain you have some soothing music on your iPod, and it just might do the trick. They'll be grateful. Slip the headphones on the baby and select Crying Baby Playlist 1, preloaded with the Coldplay album of your choice.

Watch as the infant immediately falls asleep to the sounds of the world's most boring band. (You might want to download a copy of Celine Dion's *Greatest Hits* too. I imagine to a baby she sounds a little bit like a warm placenta.)

Crying Baby Playlist 2: Ages Three Through Five

The brains are a little bigger at this age. Unfortunately, short-term memories and attention spans are still a little lacking. They've been told by their parents that if they quit crying, they'll get to go to Disney World and see Mickey Mouse. (Whether or not this is true is inconsequential.) The parents are tired of hissing "behave" every two seconds, and they have grown immune to their children's crying. You, on the other hand, have not. You're going to need to help keep the little buggers focused on their destination. For a little help, load Playlist 2, with the two most repetitive songs in Disney history: "It's a Small World" and "Be Our Guest," the song the candlestick and everyone sings in *Beauty and the Beast.*

Crying Baby Playlist 3: Ages Five Through Seven

At this age children's minds are fully developed, and you have to be a little more creative. Offer to let a crying kid watch your video iPod for a little while. Smile at the useless parents, and tell them you've got a TV show that calms down your niece and nephew every time they watch it.

On the screen a *Barney* episode will start playing. The parents will smile approvingly at everybody's favorite purple dinosaur, then go back to reading their *Bad Parenting* magazine. After a few moments, your prerecorded voiceover with the following message will begin playing while the Barney show continues:

(Read in a sinister voice.) *Hey kid. Yeah, that's right. I'm talking to you. Listen, this ain't Barney. This is Barney's evil twin brother, Ron. This is not a joke. You say one word to your mom and this whole plane is going down.*

This is no ordinary iPod. Inside are 1,000 megabytes of kryptonite, which at any moment can be released from the battery compartment in the back. If you move so much as one inch in your chair or make one sound, everyone on board will die.

This episode is set on endless repeat. If it shuts off before the plane lands, you have three seconds to restart it before it explodes in your hands.

Remember. Brother Ron will be watching you.

Continue smiling when the kid looks up to you in sheer horror, and give him a little wink and rustle his hair. Kids, they really are the future.[27]

Tips for Avoiding Crying Babies when Selecting Your Seat

- Choose exit rows whenever possible. Children under the age of fifteen aren't allowed to sit in exit rows. Suckas.
- Don't choose a connecting flight through Orlando, Florida during school vacation week. (Or any city within two hundred miles of a Disney theme park or Six Flags amusement park).
- Pick single middle seats. You may be cramped, but chances are you'll be seated between two single adult passengers (who hopefully don't cry).
- Avoid selecting a window seat in an empty row. You may think you're giving yourself the best chance of being able to stretch out across all the seats and sleep the entire flight, but if you read the previous section on overbooking, you know this is pretty much a pipe dream. And guess who is going to be coming in right next to you? Yup, crying-baby family.

---

27. If a kid is still crying on airplanes past age eight, just take him to the back of the plane and lock him in the lavatory. Yes, it's wrong, and yes you might go to jail, but you'll be a local hero. And often, local heroes have to sacrifice their freedom for the safety and well-being of others.

HOW TO SURVIVE A SUDOKU ATTACK

We've all been there. The ten-year-old seated next to you has ripped through an entire book of super-advanced, black belt–level Sudokus while munching on a bag of pretzels, playing Game Boy in his left hand, and blasting the tunes from his iPod in his right. You've been staring at the in-flight magazine for two hours and can't get a single number filled in on your large print puzzle for gentle beginners. And just when you think you can't take anymore, the passenger on the other side of you leans over, glances at your unfinished puzzle and casually reminds you that, "Knowing where a number *can't* go is just as valuable as knowing where it *can* go." Before you inform your fellow passenger precisely where they can go, take a break from logic hell and read this section. (Then you can return to your puzzle and carry on with your nervous breakdown.)

NAKED SINGLES, NAKED PAIRS, CAGES, FORBIDDING CHAINS . . . WORLD'S MOST ADDICTIVE LOGIC PUZZLE, OR KINKY SEX CLUB?

Type the word *Sudoku* into Google and you'll get more than a staggering sixty million hits. Open any strategy guide and you'll find yourself quickly lost among an underground world of single candidates, naked pairs, naked triplets, tips on how to properly bootstrap locked candidates, or how to solve for three in a bed.[28] (Careful searching for that particular tip on the Internet at work.)

A Brief History of Sudoku

2800 BC: Sandal-wearing dudes come up with Magic Squares Game while killing time waiting for the next camel to arrive at Mesopotamia International Airport.

1976 AD: Modern version of Sudoku game invented in the United States by Howard Garnes, a seventy-four-year-old retired puzzle constructor.

1980s: Japan catches wind of the game, and as with most American inventions, comes up with a way to make it better and faster.

2004: The *London Times* publishes its first Sudoku puzzle.

2005: The *New York Post* publishes the first Sudoku puzzle in the United States, making the puzzle's twenty-year round-trip journey back to the United States complete.

2008: I throw a party after finally beating my ex-fiancé at a Sudoku puzzle, at which point she promptly loses interest in the game, and subsequently calls off our wedding.

Clearly, Sudoku has surpassed the crossword puzzle and the word search as the resident favorite of in-flight magazines and puzzle books in airport terminals worldwide. The twisted little 9 x 9 square logic puzzle has been responsible for passengers missing their connecting flights, cost people their jobs, put plans for procreation on hold, and

---

28. If all this is starting to get you hot and bothered, keep in mind every bit of research was written by nerdy mathematicians with tape on their glasses, who were supposed to be solving the global warming crisis..

yes, broken up many a relationship in which one partner has proven to have a far better grasp on the game than the other. It's an evil, evil little game. So why even bother? Because the feeling of finally completing a Sudoku puzzle is a euphoric high more addictive than cigarettes, sex, and the world's best recreational drugs combined. And if history has taught us anything, it's that humans will do pretty much anything for a euphoric high.

In fact, so much excitement and sheer pandemonium has surrounded this logic puzzle phenomenon that I felt it warranted its own special supplemental section—because no one deserves to be beaten by a ten-year-old at everything.

TIPS FOR BEATING THAT GODD%#N SUDOKU ONCE AND FOR ALL

If your IQ test revealed that perhaps you won't be finding a cure for cancer this year, don't worry. I'm sure you still have a lot to offer society with your puppet shows and your warm smile. But you can still enjoy Sudoku just like everyone else, starting with these basic tips. (And be sure to complete the Sudoku Confidence Booster at the end of this chapter.)

- Use a pencil *and* an eraser.
- Write the numbers 1 through 9 on a separate piece of paper so you can refer to it for potential answers whenever needed. (By the same token you may want to list out the alphabet when you are playing along with the *Wheel of Fortune* at home. Those vowels can be tricky.)
- Use a blank piece of paper to block off the part of the puzzle you're not working on so you don't get easily distracted.

- Don't cut off your thumb so you only have nine fingers to make keeping track of the numbers easier. Just paint your extra thumbnail black, or cover it with a SpongeBob Band-Aid.

- If you get completely stumped, log on to Sudoku-solutions.com and input as many numbers as you've already solved, then click Hint. Is this cheating? Yes. (But it will be our little secret.)

- Be sure to reward yourself with a nice ice cream after you complete your first puzzle. You earned it!

Do You Care?:
What's In a Name?

- The puzzle's original name was Suuji Wa Dokushin Ni Kagiru, which means "the numbers must be single." Thankfully, this was changed to the much hipper Sudoku by a rather prudent Japanese businessman.

- The total number of possible solutions for a 9 × 9 Sudoku grid is 6,670,903,752,021,072,936,960, which is roughly the number of micrometers (one-millionth of a meter) to the nearest star (give or take a few). Strangely, 6,670,903,752,021,072,936,960 to 1 also represents the exact odds that you will ever get laid if you waste your time trying to calculate this number.

WHEN ALL ELSE FAILS, MIKE BRADY WILL KNOW JUST WHAT TO DO

Maybe you're like me. I'm no good with numbers. I used to be, but somewhere along the line the capacity (and desire) to process numbers escaped me. But, I'm real good at looking at pictures. Open your inflight magazine to the Sudoku page. Take a look at the puzzle. Nine rows across, nine rows down, separated into 3 x 3 cubes. Remind you of anything? Nothing? How about a story about a lovely lady, bringing up three very lovely girls?

Now look again.

You'll note that the nine squares in each of the 3 x 3 grids within the puzzle correspond exactly with the nine squares shown at the beginning and end of every *Brady Bunch* episode, comprised by the members of the Brady family. To solve any Sudoku puzzle, all you will need to do is assign a member of the Brady family to each of the numbers 1 through 9, as illustrated in the chart below. Then, simply arrange the pictures so there is exactly one member of the family in each row and column, and a complete family in each square: A man named Brady, his wife, three girls with hair of gold, three boys of his own, and a menopausal housekeeper named Alice.

Follow the simple chart, and guaranteed you will be solving Sudokus in no time at all![29]

---

29.   If you are not familiar with the *Brady Bunch* TV show, simply substitute any other large TV show family in their place. The cast of *Eight Is Enough*, *The Cosby Show*, *Full House* (if you include Uncle Jessie's band members from Jessie and the Rippers) or *Star Trek: The Next Generation* (if you include Ensign Wesley Crusher before he lost his boyish charm and they wrote him off) will all do nicely.

Sudoku-to–Brady Family Conversion Chart

1 - Marcia	4 - Carol	7 - Greg
2 - Jan	5 - Alice	8 - Peter
3 - Cindy	6 - Mike	9 - Bobby

Substitutes: Sam the Butcher, Cousin Oliver

If you are more of a sports person, consider using the greatest team in sports history, the World Champion 2004 Boston Red Sox, who came back from a 3–0 deficit to beat the New York Yankees in the American League Playoffs, and went on to break the curse of the Bambino and win their first World Series in eighty-five years, conveniently listed below by batting order.

Sudoku-to–2004 Red Sox Conversion Chart

1 - Johnny Damon (CF)	4 - Manny Ramirez (LF)	7 - Kevin Millar (RF)
2 - Mark Bellhorn (2B)	5 - Nomar Garcia parra (SS)	8 - Bill Mueller (3B)
3 – David Ortiz (DH)	6 - Jason Varitek (C)	9 - Pokey Reese (2B)

Did Jan Brady Let You Down Once Again?

Sudoku still got you stressed out? Try Roku Duko, Sudoko's younger cousin, which are easier puzzles made up of 6 x 6 squares. Still stumped? Shi Doku, also known as Junior Doku, are 4 x 4 grids, often used to introduce kindergarteners to numbers. If this still proves too challenging, try sitting in your seat quietly and have someone bring the tray table down for you, then work on getting it back into its upright position before the plane lands.

Hug Me Bonus Game 1: Sudoku Term or U.S. Military Operation?

For each term listed below, determine if the word or words refer to the game of Sudoku, or a U.S. military operation. Award one point for each correct answer. Award two bonus points if you participated in the military operation (and a heartfelt thank you for your service to the country). Deduct fifteen points if you were the military commander or super nerd responsible for coming up with any of these words.

1. X-wing
2. Skyscraper
3. Eagle Claw
4. Nonet
5. Flaming Dart

6. X-wing
7. Skyscraper
8. Eagle Claw
9. Nonet
10. Flaming Dart

Answers: *1. Sudoku. 2. Sudoku. 3. Military. 4. Sudoku. 5. Military. 6. Sudoku. 7. Sudoku. 8. Military. 9. Sudoku. 10. Both (although only used as a military term in fictional movie with the same name).*

Hug Me Bonus Game 2: Sudoku Confidence Booster

Here is a puzzle to get you started. Using all of the methods you have learned, complete the following Sudoku. Take as much time as necessary.

6	5	9	1	4	2	7	3	8
1	7	8	3	5	9	4	6	2
2	3	4	7	6	8	9	5	1
5	9	6	4	3	1	2	8	7
4	2	3	8		6	5	1	9
8	1	7	9	2	5	6	4	3
3	8	2	6	9	4	1	7	5
9	4	1	5	8	7	3	2	6
7	6	5	2	1	3	8	9	4

Can't Get Enough?

The following are some additional recommended resources for the Sudokolly-insane:

- Dailysudoku.com
- Sudoku.com

- Sodoku.org.uk
- Sudoku-solutions.com
- Websodoku.com

And about 59 million others.

CHAPTER 6

STILL IN THE AIR

There are only two reasons to sit in the back row of an airplane: Either you have
diarrhea, or you're anxious to meet people who do.   —Henry Kissinger

If you've flown recently, did it feel like something was missing? Was
there something about your onboard experience that was lacking?
Like you just watched another entire episode of *Will & Grace* and you
couldn't find a plot? Chances are, it was the in-flight snacks that were
to blame.

Imagine being at a Catholic mass and going up to receive Holy
Communion when suddenly, instead of receiving the little Body of
Christ cookie as has been the custom for the past two thousand years,
you find a chalice full of raisins. That's pretty much what the airlines
have pulled on us with the removal of free peanuts from most flights.
Oh, they've tried to fool us by installing private TVs in every seat and
offering all sorts of other snack options. JetBlue, for instance, has a
snack menu of eight different items available for purchase. But a $3 bag
of Terra Blues Chips or Mrs. GoodCookie Jungle Crackers is not going
to fool us on what's really happening here: We're getting jacked.

WHAT HAPPENED TO THE PEANUTS?

Remember the days when airlines used to serve peanuts on every flight?
Remember the little honey-roasted nuggets of pure sodium and endless

joy? Tiny bags of happiness that made you feel like you were enjoying the afternoon at the ball game, and not stuck in the middle seat between two sumo wrestlers for the length of a cross-country flight?

Sadly, most airlines have done away with the happiness peanuts provides and replaced them with their cheaper, low-fat cousin, the pretzel. Pretzels are not fun. Pretzels taste like cardboard. Cardboard does not make you feel like you're at a ball game. Cardboard makes you sad.

Unfortunately, it looks like cousin pretzel is here to stay.

In 1998, the Department of Transportation passed a law requiring airlines to establish a peanut-free buffer zone of three rows surrounding any passenger with a medically documented peanut allergy. Peanut allergies can be extremely serious, and even airborne peanut dust can trigger a severe reaction among sufferers. After dealing with these restrictions for years, along with the increased pressure from health advocacy groups demanding healthier snacks for lazy Americans, many airlines decided it was far easier to just serve pretzels, no matter how much they suck.

I have no problem with ensuring the safety of peanut-allergy sufferers, but I do believe this to be unfair discrimination. I, for instance, am allergic to crying babies. If peanut-allergy suffers are entitled to a peanut-free zone, I should be entitled to a crying baby–free zone.

Thankfully, you should always be able to get your honey-roasted fix when you fly Southwest, a company that built its entire marketing campaign around "flying for peanuts." Flying for pretzels really doesn't pack the same punch. (And don't worry if you are a peanut-allergy sufferer. Southwest will still remove peanuts from an entire flight if you ask. Safety first, snack foods second.)

Peanut Fun Facts

- Southwest routinely swaps out their honey-roasted peanuts with regular peanuts every six months due to the higher cost of the honey-roasted variety.

- The term *peanut gallery* originated in the late nineteenth century, and referred to the cheap, uppermost seats in the back of a theater from where rowdy patrons threw peanuts at performers on stage, stating their displeasure over a particular scene. No wonder the phantom of the opera started wearing that mask on his face to protect him from the assault.

- Americans eat eight hundred million pounds of peanut butter each year, or enough to cover the floor of the Grand Canyon.

- Reduced-fat peanut butter is not as healthy for you as you may think. While reduced-fat varieties have slightly less fat than regular peanut butter (which can contain as many calories as a Burger King hamburger), they contain more sugar, and a higher amount of hydrogenated vegetable oil (bad fat). Your best bet? All-natural, organic peanut butter, which is high in healthy monounsaturated fats that lower your cholesterol. But either will work if you're spreading it on the Grand Canyon.

- The very first *Peanuts* cartoon strip was published on October 2, 1950. Charles Schultz wasn't too happy United Feature Syndicate changed his original name from "Li'l Folks," but he happily accepted the $90 paycheck. Yep, Schultz initially only received $90 for what eventually became the most famous cartoon strip in the world. Good Grief.

> • Everyone knows Jimmy Carter was called the Peanut President due to his early career as a peanut farmer. Ah, but did you know there was also another peanut farmer turned U.S. president? Good ol' Thomas Jefferson. I can guarantee that if either Tommy or Jimmy C. were still in office, we would not be having this pretzel problem.

CURE JET LAG WITH SOME SIMPLE TRICKS

There is nothing worse than landing somewhere at midnight when your exhausted friends or family come to pick you up and you are all wired and ready to whip out the glow sticks and go raving. Or alternatively, there's nothing worse than being unable to keep from nodding off during a midday business meeting and having your coworkers draw a funny mustache on you as you drool on your laptop.

Jet lag, technically referred to as desynchronosis, is a physiological condition resulting from alterations to the body's circadian rhythms. Traveling across time zones can wreak havoc with your internal clock, and it can generally take one day to recover from each zone you cross. Of course, by the time you finally adjust, your vacation will likely be over.

The best way to combat jet lag is to ride your bicycle across the country, or sail across the ocean in a small boat to give your body ample time to adjust to each new time zone. If you insist on flying, try the following:

■ Move your watch forward to the time zone you will be landing in the moment you board the plane. If you aren't particularly good at math, glance at the watches on most flight attendants. They will likely have them already set to the new time zone.

- Eat your meals in accordance with your new time zone. Just because they are serving dinner now, doesn't mean you have to eat it now. Meals are generally served in relation to the time on the ground. Don't give in to peer pressure.

- Watch what you eat. Avoid caffeine and foods high in sugar or any other foods that might disrupt your sleep pattern. For instance, I know if I eat a banana before bedtime, I will have nightmares. I do not want nightmares on a plane, because people would be horrified to wake up and find me screaming next to them. Goes without saying, when flying, I avoid bananas.

- If you are traveling on a red-eye, sleep can often prove difficult. Be sure to follow your bedtime routine just as you would at home. Brush your teeth, get into your comfy PJs, grab your teddy bear, and watch some Letterman or your favorite late-night infomercials. If you are accustomed to getting intimate with your spouse on a nightly basis before you nod off, proceed to page 125, "Let's Get It On: Joining the Mile-High Club."

57 Channels (And Nothin' On)

The title refers to an old Bruce Springsteen song written back before fifty-seven channels of ESPN Classic barely qualifies as the bare minimum for basic cable. But it still rings true. While it's nice to have all these options for satellite and digital TV when we fly, the problem with watching television on an airplane is that there is always the temptation to see what everyone else is watching. If you peer over the row in front of you, you can see over a hundred in-seat TVs at once—each one with shows that look far better than the one you've selected. You could easily spend the entire flight flipping around, trying to catch up on every single program at the same time. And inevitably, right when your favorite sports team is about to score, or CSI: Planet Saturn is about to solve the murder of an alien stripper using a DNA sample taken from a half-eaten donut, or the panda that was trapped in the town well is about to be rescued, that little blue screen that reads "Normal Movement of the Aircraft is Causing a Temporary Loss of Signal" will rear its ugly head, and you'll miss the crucial climax of your show.

I don't really have a solution, or anything to say here, really. I just wanted to challenge myself to work Bruce Springsteen, an alien stripper, a half-eaten donut, and a panda trapped in a well into the same paragraph.

ACHOO! GRRR . . . WHY DO I GET SICK EVERY SINGLE TIME I FLY?

There is nothing worse than being trapped next to someone with the whooping cough or a steady stream of mucus flowing from their nose to their tray table for hours on end. But sometimes everyone on your flight appears healthy, yet no matter how many times you wash your hands or cover your face and breathe through your sweatshirt, you still end up feeling like death by the time you get to baggage claim. So what's going on?

Most people blame getting sick when traveling on the recycled air inside the cabin, but cabin air is surprisingly clean. It passes through a special filtration system that removes dust, vapors, bacteria, and mold, leaving it as clean or cleaner than the air inside most office buildings. However, the air on board an airplane is taken in through the jet engines, which makes it incredibly hot and dry. Additionally, humidity levels are kept low to avoid corrosion on the infinite number of metal parts on an airplane and to decrease the risk of bacteria. This lack of humidity causes you to become easily dehydrated and wreaks havoc with your sinuses. Add to this the low level of oxygen in the air, cabin pressurization, the stress of flying, and the lack of peanuts, and it's easy to see how this often leads to headaches, dizziness, feelings of nausea, and fatigue. And as the body's immune system becomes weakened, it becomes more susceptible to viruses from other passengers.

Thankfully, newer aircraft like Boeing's 787 Dreamliner are implementing drastically different airflow systems, which will create cleaner air, a higher level of oxygen, and adjustable levels of humidity based on the number of passengers on board. But until every plane in the world is modernized, here are some tips to staying healthy when traveling.

- **Lock yourself inside a human bubble.** They are relatively inexpensive, although some airlines may count a bubble as a carry-on and charge you an extra fee.

- **Drink more water than you can possibly handle.** A lot of people avoid drinking water while flying because they don't want to deal with the hassle of having to use the lavatory on the plane. *BAD IDEA.* Keeping hydrated boosts the immune system. Far better to risk peeing your pants than to let yourself become dehydrated. Do you notice your hands or feet swelling when you fly? That's your body telling you it doesn't trust you to handle even this simple task, so it's taken upon itself to store water within its cells. Eight glasses of water are recommended for a regular day. If you are flying, drink a minimum of 172 glasses of water. Add another 20 if you've sucked down several bags of salty pretzels.

- **Don't drink too much caffeine or alcohol.** While caffeine and alcohol will potentially relax you, and help you come up with witty things to say to the pretty girl sitting next to you (who mentioned she has a boyfriend but from the sounds of it things aren't going too well with him), this will also dehydrate you.

- **Chill out, dude**. One of the main reasons people get sick while traveling has nothing to do with the air quality in the plane. It's the physical state of their own bodies. High levels of stress, lack of sleep, and poor diet all work together to lower the immune system. Do what you can to get as much sleep the night before your flight, and be sure to skip the airport McDonald's for a decent meal— unless you want to die.

- **Bring your own pillow with you when you fly**. Charlie Brown's little gay friend, Linus, had this one right. Sorry to inform you, but there aren't washing machines on board airplanes. And it can often take several days for the flight attendants to manage to save up enough quarters to take everything to the Laundromat. Unless you remove a pillow or blanket from a sealed bag, just assume it has been slept on, drooled on, sneezed on, and stuffed down someone else's pants for several flights prior to yours. (I've never actually seen someone stuff a blanket down their pants, but it's best not to take the risk.)

- **Try nasal irrigation, also known as neti-potting**. Rinsing the nasal cavity with salt water or a saline wash before and after flying can clear away allergens, irritants, bacteria, and viruses from the nose. Many singers use this technique in order to keep their head free from congestion. If you feel your karaoke career is worth it, by all means go ahead.

And if you are sick yourself, please don't fly. We don't want to hate you, but if you cough all over us, we will.

SKIP THE SUDAFED, GET ADJUSTED

Really want to do all you can to avoid getting sick every time you fly? Visit your chiropractor. Decades of studies have proven that regular chiropractic care will help keep the immune system functioning at 100 percent and greatly enhance the body's natural ability to ward off sickness. By keeping the spinal column aligned, pressure on the nervous system is alleviated, which allows the free flow of energy throughout the body, allowing the immune system to do its thing. And should you manage to catch the sniffles, a well-adjusted body will be able to ward off a cold far faster than an unhealthy one. Combine that with a healthy diet full of fruits and vegetables, a few vitamins, and a little luck that you didn't get seated directly next to the bird-flu guy, and at least now you've got a fighting chance.

This Ain't Denny's

Remember, an airplane is not a restaurant (or an intensive care unit). Do not ring your call button for every little thing. You are not the only person on the plane, and flight attendants don't work on tips.[30] This means not asking for a cup of coffee the moment you sit down, when there is severe turbulence, or when the flight attendant is trapped behind the beverage cart. You might think this doesn't bother them because they deliver your drinks with a smile each and every time. But trust me, it does.

---

30.   If you don't think a flight attendant's job is difficult, imagine being the only worker in charge of the drive-thru at McDonald's, having to serve hot coffee during an earthquake without spilling a single drop to a line of customers stretching endlessly for miles. And remember, if you don't smile, "You're fired!"

EXPLODING EARS—MAKE THEM STOP!

There they go again. Pop. Pop. Pop. My ears feel like they just exploded inside my head. But we're barely off the ground. God I hate flying. What's going on here?

Airplane cabins are pressurized to maintain a suitable living environment for human beings (and small pets) while cruising around at thirty thousand feet, where it's flippin' cold and there ain't much air. While it would be nice to have this living environment equal to the air pressure at ground level, this would require an incredibly heavy fuselage to withstand the outward forces placed upon it, making for one insanely impractical airplane that would cost millions to fly.

Instead, airplane cabins are pressurized to a simulated altitude of five thousand to eight thousand feet, which is why your ears can pop right away as you adjust from ground level up. This is also why you may notice babies crying during takeoffs and landings, which is due to their little baby eustachian tubes being so narrow they get easily blocked. (This is the only time you need to feel bad for a crying baby.)

Okay, dammit. Now I want them to pop and they won't. Help!

The pain from a blocked tube can be quite intense, especially if you are suffering from allergies or a cold. If chewing gum and swallowing isn't cutting it, the best method for getting your ears to pop is to pinch your nose and close your mouth while forcibly exhaling through your nostrils to equalize the pressure inside your ear, commonly known as the Valsalva maneuver. You may also want to bend over and place your head between your legs when you attempt this. This has little do to with relieving the pressure, but is a precautionary measure so you don't accidentally blow boogers over everyone in your row.

Screw this. They're still killing me. What else you got?

Believe it or not, unlike the companies who design cramped airplane seats, there are folks out there who care about your discomfort when flying. Do your ears a favor, and pick up a pack of EarPlanes at your local drugstore. EarPlanes are special ear plugs designed to relieve pressure within the ear by restricting the flow of air to the eardrum and giving the inner ear more time to compensate for changes in pressure. They will also reduce engine noise, and help to drown out crying babies. If you can't find EarPlanes, you can try standard earplugs, although you need to make sure they form a complete seal around the ear canal or they'll be useless. Be sure to put them in before you take off, and don't remove them until you've reached your full cruising altitude. Or if you happen to be fighting with your wife, perhaps leave them in the entire flight: "SORRY HUN! CAN'T HEAR YOU RIGHT NOW! GOT MY EARPLANES IN! WHAT'S THAT? SOUNDS LIKE YOU'RE SAYING YOU WERE WRONG AND YOU WANT TO APOLOGIZE? OF COURSE, I'LL FORGIVE YOU. WHAT? NO, I HAVEN'T SEEN THE KIDS SINCE WE WENT THROUGH SECURITY. I THOUGHT THEY WERE WITH YOU. WHAT?! CAN'T HEAR YOU. WHY DON'T YOU STOP SHOUTING AND WORK ON YOUR SUDOKU? YOU'RE BEING RUDE TO THE OTHER PASSENGERS."

SKYMALL SHOPPING

I know none of you would ever be so thoughtless as to wait until the last minute to buy a present for the relatives you're visiting and rely on SkyMall to rush a package to their door before you hit the ground. In fact, I know none of you would even consider it, because never once in all my years of flying have I seen someone order a single item from this catalog. My only theory of its existence is there was a government mandate established in the '70s requiring each seatback to contain one copy in order to quell panic attacks of women discovering they won't be able to shop for five hours during cross-country flights.

Did the Engines Fall Off? Was the Plane Boarded by Aliens? What the Hell Was That Noise?

No doubt anyone who has flown at least once could likely step in and make a fairly thorough preflight safety announcement, should all the flight attendants suffer laryngitis simultaneously. (Could happen.) But what do all the little noises mean? How do I know when to pick up the phone? Are we in some sort of giant flying elevator? Is the coffee done brewing?

- A single BING. Passenger pressed his or her flight attendant call button.
- BING-Bong. Pilot ringing the flight attendant's phone.
- BING-Bong. BING-Bong. Informs flight attendants it's time to prepare the cabin for landing.
- BING BING BING BING. Pilot has fallen asleep at the wheel.

Additionally, flight attendants may sound like they're talking in code, but it's pretty simple. Things like "1LR/2LR secure," simply refer to the status of the doors on the left and right side of the plane, just as "Em Land, Nut Out" signals the pilot the plane needs to make an emergency landing, we are out of peanuts.

If you are stepping in to make the announcements on a flight, you may want to verify the doors are actually secured and the plane is ready to take off before picking up the intercom. Just to be safe.

But just in case you "accidentally" bought any of the following items from a SkyMall catalog after turning in one-too-many free-drink coupons and going on a blitzed buying binge, I am offering you a chance at redemption if you agree to donate the purchase price of your item (plus shipping and handling) to the charity of your choice.

SkyMall Items for Which You Need to Pay Your Penance for Ordering

Star Trek Full-size Captain's Chair: $2,717.01

Really? How mad at the wife were you when you decided to max out your credit card and have this little baby delivered while she was spending the night at her sister's? Unless you bought this *only* as a prop for fantasy night when you play Captain Kirk and your lady plays Lieutenant Uhura (or that hot green alien chick), you best write a $2,717.01 check out to charity pronto. Because there is no living room in America where this chair is acceptable décor.

State-of-the-art Breathalyzer: $199

Here's a hint. If you need a two-hundred dollar breathalyzer to tell you if you are okay to drive, you are not okay to drive. In fact, you are an idiot. Make a double donation to charity if you bought this product. Triple donation if you bought one as a gift for your teenager when he got his driver's license.

53-Battery Storage Center: $14.99

If you have time to organize fifty-three batteries in their own little slots, you really need to be doing more on a daily basis to help society.

Digital Photo Keychain: $39.95

Unless you have Alzheimer's so bad you can't remember what your car looks like when you park it, there is no justification for this purchase.

Congratulations. Thieves will now know exactly what all your children look like when they steal your car from the valet.

Towel-matic Touchless Dispenser: $59.99

Dispenses paper towels with the wave of your hand. Identifies perforations and stops right on the line each time. Didn't your mom teach you to avoid anything with the word towel-matic in it? Again, technology we don't need and didn't ask for.

Doggie Lawn Chair: $34.99

No. We're already following them around with little bags and picking up their poop. Why not just give them the keys to the car and a seat on the senate?

The Indoor Dog Restroom Artificial Green Turf and Pee Tray System: $149.95

No. (See above.)

Cat-shaped Heated Neck Pillow: $39.95

No. You might as well just board the plane wearing your crocs and your fanny pack and check your genitals through to your final destination, because you won't be needing them ever again.

GETTING THE CUTE FLIGHT ATTENDANT'S NUMBER, EACH AND EVERY TIME

It's a known fact that all women want men to take an interest in their careers. Ask any woman a question about her job and watch her eyes light up and her speech pattern take on the speed of a frenzied gazelle.[31]

---

31. I considered this analogy very carefully because I in no way want to insult the female race here. I was just looking for a cute animal that maybe would be chatty if it were asked about its career. I meant it as a compliment. I love chatty women. Really, I love them just as much as I love gazelles. They make great pets. Not that I think women are pets. Nor do I think they belong in a zoo, or in any kind of cage at all. That's crazy talk. Oh my God. Is it getting hot in here or is that just me?

Do You Care?

Southwest Airlines offers complimentary alcohol on select holidays. Actually, just two holidays: Finlandia Vodka on Valentine's Day and your choice of beer on St. Patrick's Day. I'm not sure what marketing message they're trying to send here. Apparently, if you're single or Irish, they feel bad and want to help.

Female flight attendants are no different. By learning a few key elements of her world, you will be far better prepared when you look up and find the woman of your dreams pushing that drink cart down the aisle. And remember, each flight is like being on a four-hour first date she can't walk away from. Use your time wisely:

- Never refer to a flight attendant as a stewardess. This is as politically incorrect as referring to Asians as Orientals, or James Blunt as a talented musician.

- Pay close attention when she gives the preflight safety speech. When she points to the nearest exits, look over and nod approvingly at her ability to describe what a door looks like.

- Don't be afraid to raise your hand and ask a question, like what is the load-bearing capacity of each engine on the 747 wide-body. It's doubtful she will have the correct answer handy, but just smile and thank her, even if she is *way* off. This will make her feel important, and show you care about airplanes and safety—an important quality if she is searching for a suitable mate for raising children. (And they all are.)

- Always be on the lookout for opportunities to help a flight attendant with her job. If you find a flight attendant you are attracted to struggling to fit an unusually large and awkward carry-on bag into the overhead compartment that some idiot just left in the aisle, rush to her side and help her lift it. (Unless it's your bag, in which case you better hope you removed your nametags.)

- Always carry a pocket full of one dollar bills on board with you. Keep them rolled up in a big wad, and wrap a twenty around the outside. When your hottie flight attendant makes an announcement to press your call button if anyone has change for a twenty, casually hit your button and pull out your roll of bills. She'll be instantly grateful (and naturally attracted to your money).

- Order a vodka and tonic and offer to buy one for her. She'll laugh and politely decline, saying she can't drink on the job. Order one anyway. In the confusion, she'll forget to charge you for it. This will help ease the pain later if she turns you down.

If you are a woman or a gay male and find yourself attracted to a male flight attendant, I think you just compliment him on his tie and he will have sex with you. At least that's what I've heard from my gay friend Jerry.

Hottest Flight Attendants Ranked by Airline

1. Lufthansa
2. United (My friend's lovely wife works for United—I have to represent.)
3. British Airways
4. Sandpiper Airlines (The little airline from *Wings*)
5. Virgin Atlantic Airlines
6. Air Canada
7. Hawaiian Air
8. Air Alaska
9. Southwest
10. UPS Air Freight Service

LET'S GET IT ON: JOINING THE MILE-HIGH CLUB (EVEN ON SOUTHWEST)

I'm sure for most couples this topic has come up from time to time at a dinner party where one too many bottles of wine were opened, or during a particularly rousing game of Pictionary. "Well, one time, when we flew to Greece for our honeymoon, Jim and I held hands under the blanket when no one was looking . . ."

Oh, my Judy, we're so impressed. Come on. The flight staff on Lufthansa holds a full orgy in the back of the plane every night. Show me a couple who can rip through an entire booklet of free-drink coupons and get it on in the one-hour flight between LA and Vegas in the middle of the afternoon on Southwest, and *now* we're talking. Read this section closely, and the next time this topic comes up in conversation, give your honey a wink and a secret smile, and be proud, Judy. Be very proud.

Mile-High Club: Initiation Instructions for the Female

Required: *loose clothing, transparent red film, Scotch tape, synchronized watches, and an iPod cued to a Justin Timberlake playlist.*

The female should be wearing a skirt or loose-fitting pants with a drawstring. If this is not possible, at least make sure you're not making matters worse with a corset or six layers of leggings. We're going for speed here, not romance.

After you are airborne, order a glass of wine (or seven) to relax, and then wait for the feature film to begin playing. When the majority of the cabin is focused on the movie, check to make sure the lavatory is unoccupied, then stand up, note the time on you and your partner's synchronized watches, and then proceed to the rear of the plane. Enter the lavatory and close the door. Do *not* look in the mirror: Unless you are sufficiently intoxicated, that little voice inside your head will be asking "Just what do you think you're doing?" and will wreck the moment.

Since the lights go on automatically when you close the lavatory door on an aircraft, and flight staff frown on passengers tampering with electrical wiring, you will need to make some minor adjustments in order to create an environment sexy enough for your encounter. First, put the lid down on the toilet seat. (This was Chevy Chase's fatal mistake in *Vegas Vacation*.) Next, reach up and place the red cellophane over the light, securing it with a piece of tape. Then sit down and put your headphones on and hit Play on your iPod. As there will be no time for foreplay, it will be your responsibility to warm yourself up for your partner.[32] Close your eyes and focus on the smooth, sexy sounds of JT while you wait for your man.

---

32. Always a good idea in general.

Mile-High Club: Initiation Instructions for the Male

Required: *appropriate contraceptive device, willing partner.*

After your travel companion leaves her seat, you will need to wait precisely seven minutes before proceeding to the lavatory love shack. Any sooner, and flight attendants may notice you sneaking off together. Any longer, and you won't be able to contain your excitement.

Use this time to mentally prepare. Take several deep breaths. Yes, this is really happening. This will be one of the only times in your life your girlfriend or wife is feeling frisky enough to try this. There can be no room for errors or early misfires. If anything goes wrong, rest assured you will not be getting another invitation to join the MH club ever again.

After six minutes and thirty seconds have passed, stand up and slowly begin walking toward the bathroom. Remain confident. Walk with a purpose. If you encounter a flight attendant en route, simply nod your head to acknowledge their presence. Do *not* smile. Smiling is a dead giveaway. Airlines tie stock options and holiday bonuses to a flight attendant's ability to successfully thwart bathroom sex offenders. Don't become a statistic.

If there is someone waiting by the door to the lavatory, don't panic. You've prepared for this. Ask the person waiting if he's sure anyone is in the lavatory. He will nod his head and point to the lit sign that reads "Occupied" (*Ocupado*). Glance at your watch, and as soon as it reads exactly seven minutes, gently press on the door. Providing you have synchronized your watches, your partner will be sliding the lock open right at this very moment, and the door will open inward. Remark that the door must have been stuck, then ask if he minds if you slip in before him, as you really, really have to go. (If he only knew how bad . . .) He will feel like such a fool for waiting so long outside of an unoccupied lavatory, he'll consent.

Open the door and quickly step inside. If everything has gone to plan, you will find a very turned-on partner illuminated in sexy red lighting, swaying her hips and lip syncing to JT's "Rock Your Body," the club mix. Do your thing.

How you exit afterward is up to you. Some couples try to be just as secretive on the return trip to their seats. Some crack out the champagne and balloons and ask the flight attendants to announce to the cabin the newest members of the world's most exciting club. It's important to remain true to your style.

In the afterglow of your mile-high accomplishment, you may want to take a moment to thank the one person who made this entire experience possible: the pilot. Be sure to tip him on the way out for the smooth ride. But first, let's take a little look at what he actual does up there.

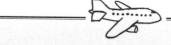

After You, My Dear

The female should always proceed to the lavatory first in the MH club initiation for a number of reasons, the most notable of which is it's always more exciting for the male to pursue the female of the species. Plus, no one is going to question a woman spending extra time in the bathroom. They will assume it may be her time of the month, or that she is giving birth. Neither will warrant a knock on the door as both can be messy.

If you are a gay couple, just send whoever normally plays the woman. Or if you both do, just flip a coin. (Again, advice given to me by my gay friend Jerry, so if you find it offensive, my apologies, but blame him. And you probably better look out if he's on your flight and you're sitting near the lavatory.)

CHAPTER 7

PILOTS, GUNS, & MONEY ... FUN WITH FLYING

How many pilots does it take to screw in a lightbulb?

Just one. He holds the bulb and the world revolves around him.

Airline Pilot: #1 Job in the World.

In 2002, the FAA passed a regulation requiring the cockpit door to remain locked for the duration of the flight on all U.S. airlines. While many viewed this as a necessary step to ensure passenger safety, it was actually just an excuse to turn the cockpit into the ultimate men's club. A nonstop, private party at thirty thousand feet, with access to any destination in the world in a matter of hours.

Ask any group of kindergartners what they want to be when they grow up, and guaranteed at least one in ten will say "airline pilot." Along with fireman, president of the United States, and personal assistant to Ray Romano, being an airline pilot is one of the most exciting careers a kid can dream of. And now, thanks to nifty computers, planes basically fly themselves. The only actual work a pilot has to do during a flight is to step in and shake the mouse on his computer should the screensaver come on. Let's face it, a commercial airline pilot can be one of the most rewarding, stress-free jobs in the world.

With so little to do as he soars through the skies, a pilot can spend countless hours watching TV, gambling with the first officer, having sex, or even running another company from a corner office with the world's most unbeatable view.

Additional benefits include

- Keys to one of the fastest vehicles on the planet
- Excuse to wear cool aviator sunglasses and not get called a tool
- Drinks and snacks are always served to you before anyone else
- High probability of being elected mayor in the event of landing on a deserted island

HAVE YOU GOT WHAT IT TAKES?

To determine if you qualify to be an airline pilot, take the following test.

Eligibility Test for Becoming a Commercial Airline Pilot

1. Do you drink coffee?
2. Do you look good in a cap?

Providing you answered yes to both of the above, you're golden. Those are the only requirements to becoming a pilot. It's an unwrit-

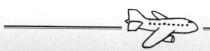

**Unrelated Facts, That Are Amusing
When Grouped Together**

- United Airlines currently employs the most female pilots in the United States, with over five hundred currently on their payroll.
- On January 13, 2008, a United Airlines 757 backed into a commuter jet in a 2 mph collision in the parking lot at San Francisco International Airport.

ten law that all pilots must enter the cockpit carrying a cup of coffee, because people trust you when you're holding a cup of coffee. "Look at Pilot Johnson holding his coffee—so confident and relaxed. He must know how to work all those controls."

Likewise, you'll need to look good in a cap when they take the annual company photo. And be sure to keep a copy. If your airline goes out of business you'll have a great headshot you can use to find a job driving a limo.

SOUNDS GOOD, BUT WHAT'S IT PAY?

According to survey statistics, the average annual commercial airline pilot salary is between $75 to $100K, which isn't too shabby. But when you break this down according to actual hours worked, it gets even better:

- Turn on the engines (two minutes)
- Inform passengers of local weather and current time (one minute)
- Relay ball game scores when flying during play-offs (two minutes)
- Point out to the main cabin passengers any celebrities flying in first class (one minute)
- Assemble tribes and lead hunt for food in the event of landing on deserted island (hours vary; overtime rate applies)

Based on the actual amount of time spent doing any real work, a domestic airline pilot earns approximately $8,337 per hour, or about $17.3 million a year. That's roughly the same amount that Mary-Kate and Ashley Olsen earn each year from managing their international line of clothing, designed exclusively for identical twin millionaire actresses and teenage vampires, for far less stress.

IT'S CALLED "COCKPIT" FOR A REASON

"Hey, hey! Let's get this party started! Whoa . . . wait a minute, where all the ladies at?" According to the International Society of Women Airline Pilots, women make up less than 5 percent of the total number of pilots worldwide. While women have pretty much equaled or surpassed men in virtually every profession in the past few decades, for some reason this remains a predominantly male-driven world.

There are many debates as to why women have yet to venture into the cockpit in mass numbers. In truth, it has little to do with a woman's physical ability or her desire to prove herself by competing against gallons of male testosterone. What really keeps her on the ground is the stress of flying over hundreds of malls everyday and not being able to stop and go inside any of them.

IMPRESS YOUR DATE: GETTING A PILOT'S LICENSE

Earning a pilot's license is easier than you may think. The FAA only requires forty hours of flying time before you are allowed to take your little private plane skyward. You can check out any number of websites listing flying schools across the country. If your dream is to cruise around in the big boys though, you're going to have to put in a little extra work.

Commercial airlines don't actually train pilots. Airlines hire candidates who have completed rigorous training at their own expense. Most commercial airline pilots have logged hundreds of hours of flying time, have completed at least one ten-week training program, and have passed intense physical and written exams before they ever step foot into a cockpit. Additionally, many come from military backgrounds,

Too Good to Be True

The Ireland-based Aer Lingus employs the highest percentage of women pilots in the world. If you don't understand why this is funny, read this out loud several times. If you still don't get it, ask a trusted friend to explain it to you (but not your mom). If you're still not sure, write me and I'll email you the explanation, along with some pamphlets on human sexuality. (I'd include it here, but we're trying to keep this clean—for the kids.)

where they've spent countless flying hours under intense battle conditions, or have at least reached level 70, "The Burning Crusade" on *World of Warcraft* for Xbox.

BECOMING A FEDERAL AIR MARSHAL (AND OTHER WAYS TO EARN FREQUENT FLYER MILES AT THE SPEED OF LIGHT)

Admit it. Every time you board a plane you play a little game with yourself to try and figure out who the secret Federal Air Marshal might be. No? Just me again? Well, that's probably smart. For obvious security reasons, you will never know the identity of an air marshal, or even which flights have marshals on board (unless they have to come out of hiding to silence a crying baby). But one thing is for sure. Air marshals are always in demand.

Do You Care?

Don't want to fly a plane, but really like telling people what to do? Consider a career as an air traffic controller. According to the FAA, you must meet the following requirements:

- Be a U.S. citizen.
- Be younger than thirty-one (in most cases)
- Pass a medical and security examination
- Have three years of progressively responsible work experience and/or a full four-year course of study leading to a bachelor's degree, or some combination of the two
- Achieve a score of at least 70 on the FAA preemployment test
- Speak English clearly enough to be understood over communications equipment

Following are some additional, helpful requirements:

- Have extensive experience using Post-it notes to keep track of multiple things at once
- Enjoy looking out the window for extended periods of time
- Be very good at *Space Invaders* for Atari

The Federal Air Marshal Program was started in 1970, and the recent expansion in airline security measures has boosted the demand for qualified applicants to an all-time high. If you wish to live out your dream of being a secret agent while helping protect the lives of your fellow Americans (a very sexy career choice), there is no better time than now. Visit usajobs.gov, where you will need to first register with Avue Technologies, the contracted vendor for human resources within the TSA, then complete the detailed application.

As you might expect with any job that hands you a gun as part of your orientation packet, the hiring process for a Federal Air Marshal position is fairly intense. You have to successfully complete a written application, a panel interview, psychological assessment, medical examination, physical test, and a comprehensive background investigation before you will be allowed to tackle people on planes.

I wanted to go through the full registration process so I could provide a firsthand account of what the application process entails, but I couldn't risk a background check, on account of some long-overdue library fines. (I'm not a fast reader.)

WANTED

Federal Air Marshal

Looking for an exciting career as a defender of the free world? Enjoy watching movies while you work? Like carrying a gun? Consider a career as a TSA Federal Air Marshal. Qualified candidates must exhibit the following:

- Strong observation skills
- Ability to sit for long hours at a time
- Ability to work independently
- Knowledge of Sudoku
- A hunger for pretzels

Full background check and physiological assessment required. For further information, visit usajobs.gov. Equal Opportunity Employer. No whackos.

OTHER WAYS TO EARN FREQUENT FLYER MILES THAT DON'T REQUIRE A GUN

Truthfully, no one should ever be paying for an airline ticket. There are enough credit card companies offering free miles, double miles, triple miles, bonus miles, mega miles, green miles, and the extra miles to keep you flying 'round the globe 'round the clock. Since we're a society of credit junkies, many of you may already be aware of the following credit card tips. Note: If you can't control yourself around the plastic, you might want to skip this section. Although, if you're going to wind up a million dollars in debt and sleeping in the gutter anyway, you might as well at least earn a free trip to Europe. (The gutters are more romantic there.)

- If you're still using a credit card that rewards you with points you can exchange for a travel mug or an all-in-one screwdriver set, do yourself a favor and dump it for a card that earns you frequent flyer points.

- Some cards like American Express will allow you to conveniently use your points on any airline, while others are tied specifically to a certain carrier. Do a little research to see what's best for you. Also see which cards will offer you a free T-shirt when you sign up. You can never have enough free T-shirts. (Speaking of which, Amex, I should now be on your list for that little nod I gave you there. Men's medium, please.)

- Use these cards for everything: groceries, gas, clothing, flat screen TVs, etc. Providing you pay off your balance each month, this is the fastest and most economical way to accumulate frequent flyer points. You'll be amazed at how quickly those points will add up. (Especially if your wife or girlfriend has expensive taste.) Additionally, most cell phone bills, cable bills, electric bills, gambling debts, and even car payments and college tuition can be paid using a credit card. Rack up those points baby!

- Pay close attention to special offers that double your points, and take advantage of them wherever you can. Additionally, many cards are tied to hotel and rental car companies. You may find you can take the whole family to Europe for less money than it would cost to take them to the movies.

Earning points for doing things you would normally do is one of the most exciting things you can experience in life. Make sure you don't miss out!

USE YOUR MILES WISELY

Just because you earn 'em doesn't always mean you can use 'em. Pay close attention to the fine print before you try to cash in your points for a flight to grandma's house two days before Christmas. Some fre-

Do You Care?

Do you have miles with six different airlines, gold status at ten different company rental car programs, thousands of points at hotels all over the world, and no clue when any of them expire? Check out Points.com. This nifty little site allows you to keep track of the all the stuff you refuse to keep track of. (You should probably add your wife's birthday, your wedding anniversary, and your kids' names while you're at it.) Points.com also allows you to share points with other members, buy more points (for those times when you're just a few miles short of a free trip), trade points, and even offers you free points just for signing up. Free points! Come on. How can you turn down free points?! (You can't.) Visit Pleasehugmeseries.com for a full list of everything else you can do with your fabulous points.

quent flyer miles can be used anytime, while some are subject to the dreaded blackout days. The rules vary from airline to airline, and can be as confusing as shopping for health insurance or a Dennis Miller monologue. But as long as you book far enough in advance and have a little patience, you should have no problem. And knowing you paid nothing for your flight while the person beside you paid hundreds of dollars will make any extra effort all the more worth it.

■ Don't waste your precious miles on short flights. Save them for the more expensive cross-country trips, or trips overseas.

■ If you can't use your miles for a particular trip, see if you can use them to upgrade to first class. You may be able to fly in style for a lot less than you think.

■ Cashing in frequent flyer miles during the holidays can be tricky. Most airlines block out the last two weeks of November and a large majority of December. Additionally, you may find an available flight, but with an inhumanely early departure time or a ten-hour layover. It's up to you whether you want to spend the time searching for a flight with six connections (of which your bags will make none) that will get you home just in time for the annual family fight in which Uncle Bob throws his beer onto the lit Christmas tree and all the presents go up in flames and you will get stuck wearing the turtleneck sweater grandma made you for the entire week, or spend the holidays eating alone at Denny's.

■ Don't wait forever until you use your points for that dream vacation. You never know when the next airline will go out of business, leaving you with six million useless points. Go somewhere already.

■ If your account remains inactive for more than a year, you may run the risk of losing your miles. If you don't have a trip scheduled anytime soon, you can keep your account active by renting a car or booking a hotel with a partner company, or making a small purchase if you have a credit card that earns you miles. Like, oh, I don't know, perhaps a little humor travel book or two for your friends.

LOST LUGGAGE, LOST CAUSE

The next time you are at the ticket counter, I want you to do something. I want you to raise your arm, and wave good-bye to your bags as they pass through the little black flaps into the great, mysterious beyond. Blow them a little kiss, and tell them you look forward to seeing them soon.

You may think your suitcase is an inanimate object and can't feel your love, but you'd be wrong. Your luggage is as much a part of you as your car, your iPod, or your youngest child—you know, the one named Michael that you sometimes refer to as Michael the Mistake when you think he's not listening, who tends to run away every month or so. Children who run away from home don't do so because they feel loved and appreciated. They do so out of neglect. Don't make this same mistake with your luggage.

As we all know, an airline has two jobs: 1) transport you to a specific destination, and 2) transport your luggage to the same destination. Most of the time they get number one right. On occasion they succeed with number two.

According to the *Air Travel Consumer Report*, which is a delightfully detailed document published monthly by the Department of Transportation, airlines report an average of five to fifteen customer baggage complaints for every one thousand bags handled. (This number is substantially higher during busy travel seasons.) That may not sound like they're doing that bad a job. Percentage-wise, heck, that's less than 1 percent. Maybe we should give them a break. You know, go a little easier on them.

Okay. Maybe we should. But consider in an average-size town, this would be the equivalent of a school bus system losing one kid a day, everyday, for the entire school year. (And that doesn't include Michael the Mistake.) No other industry could perform as badly, and not be shut down by whatever government agency shuts down poorly performing industries.

Of course, as with all the other depressing statistics presented here, there are ways to help push yourself over to the happy side of the fence:

- **Buy a suitcase in any color other than black.** Ninety-nine percent of all luggage worldwide is black. If you don't want yours to get lost in the shuffle, try Fuschia, or SpongeBob yellow. Unless of course you have ugly clothes and are hoping to mistakenly swap out your suitcase with someone who has a much better sense of fashion than you.

- **Put your address inside** *everything*, **along with a printed copy of your itinerary.** Consider offering a reward for the safe return of your items. You certainly aren't going to pay it, since people should not be rewarded for simply doing their job correctly, but it might get that airline van out to your house in the dead of winter a tad faster. (Okay, maybe give them a buck or two. Or that turtleneck sweater grandma gave you.)

- **Take a picture of your packed suitcase right before you zip it up.** Besides taking pictures of a guy or girl who gives you their number while you are drunk at a club so you can remember what they look like the next morning, this is probably the only useful feature of a cell phone camera. In the event your luggage goes bye-bye, you can accurately report everything you lost, without having to rely on your failing memory.

- **Never leave the ticket counter until you see** *with your very own eyes* **the agent place your bag on the belt and you watch your bag pass**

through the little black flaps. Just because there is a moving belt and a suitcase next to it does not mean the two will connect. Recall Newton's law of physics: things at rest tend to stay at rest. (Or was that your roommate's motto for your entire freshman year at college?)

■ **Whatever you do, do** *not* **piss off the ticket agent in charge of putting the tags on your luggage.** You may think this is foolish. What employee would take out his frustrations on a customer by purposely mis-tagging a bag? Well, if your faith in humanity is so great that you assume you can treat everyone as you please and nothing bad will come of it, far be it from me to warn you. And by all means, continue to send back your food every time you're in a restaurant. Be sure to yell at the cook and tell him he should be working at Popeye's. Enjoy that special salad dressing.

■ **Tape a business card to the inside of your laptop.** According to a recent study by the Ponemon Institute, an average of sixteen laptops are left at security checkpoints each day.[33] Chances are, if you haven't left a computer behind after being distracted by a gorgeous girl or a hunky guy struggling to get their clothes back on after being strip-searched, you will. In fact, tape business cards to your children while you're at it. And if you are worried no one will bother to track you down because your laptop is so old you're still running Windows '98, well, you're probably right.

■ **Pull a Clooney.** If you are embarrassed by the job title on your business card or don't like putting your personal information on the outside of your belongings, write down a celebrity name, or better yet tape a picture of a celebrity on your laptop and write your home address underneath. If it gets lost, people will be more apt

---

33. Unsurprisingly, the two airports with the highest number of reported abandoned laptops are Los Angeles International (LAX) and Miami International (MIA), two cities with the highest concentration of beautiful women passing through security, distracting the hell out of everyone. I love LA.

to deliver it right to your door on the off-chance they get to meet Mr. George Clooney or Ms. Claudia Schiffer. This will also help your laptop stand out in the bin of six hundred other lost laptops if you've decorated it with a picture of the best-looking actor in America or a nice bikini model.

If money is no object, consider shipping your luggage to your destination ahead of time. Yes, it costs more, but with airlines charging fees now for every bag you take, the extra expense may not seem so bad. Additionally, you can travel with the added peace of mind of knowing your luggage is being tracked and is insured against loss or damages. And best of all, you can jump on and off the moving sidewalks at the airport as many times as you like without having a zillion bags weighing you down. (Of course, if money is really no object, you can buy a private plane or have a cabana boy ride along beside you to carry all your stuff.)

Most shipping companies work pretty much the same. They will e-mail you or fax you preprinted shipping labels, then pick your luggage up at your door. You pay by the pound. Your luggage is generally insured up to $500 or $1000, and you can purchase additional insurance if you're shipping gold bricks or that irreplaceable afghan grandma knitted you with her arthritic hands (although you really shouldn't let that out of your sight). Some companies will even waive shipping charges and cover your daily expenses up to $500 a day if your luggage arrives late. Just like an airline will— ha, ha! Feel free to check out the following list of some of these companies:

- Luggageforward.com
- Luggagefree.com
- Theluggageclub.com

- Sportsexpress.com. (Doesn't have "luggage" in the company name, but they acquired a company called Luggage Express, so it's all good.)

- And don't forget UPS. They run the tightest ship in the shipping business.

REUNITED AND IT FEELS SO GOOD: GET THAT TINY BLACK BACKPACK BACK

Why should one ever visit the dusty town of Scottsboro, Alabama? Well, to reunite with your long-lost pal, your luggage, of course. Nestled amongst the foothills of the Appalachian Mountains you will find the world's greatest flea market, otherwise known as Unclaimed Baggage Center. If you're lucky, this is where you will find your missing suitcase.

How big is this operation? More than one million unclaimed items pass through the doors of Unclaimed Baggage each year. The facilities cover more than a city block, and come complete with their own Starbucks, Dippin' Dots, and a concierge desk to guide you through the mazes of clothes, jewelry, cameras, and secondhand treasures.

According to the website, unclaimed luggage arrives at their front door after "at least ninety days of intensive tracking by the airlines" to try to find the rightful owner. "Intensive" may be debatable, but hey, someone else's loss may be your gain, unless it's your loss, in which case, well, sorry. Either way, Unclaimed Baggage can provide a staggering amount of holiday gift ideas if you are shopping on a budget:

- iPods preloaded with thousands of songs

- Digital cameras loaded with pictures of a better-looking family

- Video cameras loaded with naughty honeymoon escapades (if you are extremely lucky)

If you are a careful shopper (and I know you are), please note swimwear, undergarments, lingerie, and food (even if you promise you didn't take a bite) are not returnable after purchase. Of course, any clothing found in a suitcase has presumably been worn before it was lost, but apparently three months in an airline storage warehouse is considered an acceptable quarantine for de-funking used gym shorts.

Here are some additional items you may encounter should you visit Unclaimed Baggage:

- Shrunken Egyptian head, found inside a Gucci suitcase
- Guidance system for an F16 fighter jet, valued at over a quarter of a million dollars
- $500 cash, found inside a Barbie doll after her head fell off
- Friendly little rattlesnake (Insert your own *Snakes on a Plane* joke here.)

ALL RIGHT, WHO THE HELL CAN I YELL AT?!

Granted, I spent a lot of time on luggage. But it's an important topic. We like our stuff, and we want to keep it. And what happens when it goes missing? Do you quietly approach the service desk and politely inquire if they have amassed any further knowledge as to the exotic destination in which your suitcase might be vacationing? Do you then chuckle in a cheeky British accent that your friend Samsonite seems to be earning more frequent flyer miles than you are this year, as you fill out your missing luggage form? I think not. (If you do, I commend you, and you have certainly earned a *Please Hug Me* Award of Excellence.)

Growing up, one of my mom's favorite sayings was, "If you don't have anything nice to say, don't say anything at all." This is probably why most of our family dinners were fairly quiet.

But of course, we all know the more modern version of this timeless proverb: "If you don't have anything nice to say, post it all over the web." Oh, we know you're angry. And you have every right to be. You didn't get the respect you deserved. Your bags didn't even end up in the same country as you. Your flight was delayed so long the people you were going to visit passed away. And no one from the airline came by to offer even the tiniest apology.

If you're going to complain, the best you can do is focus your energy where it might do some good. Log on to http://airconsumer.ost.dot .gov (no www on that bad boy), where you can find specific telephone numbers for the department matching your particular complaint type (e.g., safety issues, service complaints, etc.). All complaints registered with this site are entered in the Department of Transportation's computerized aviation industry–monitoring system and are included in the monthly *Air Travel Consumer Report*, which is distributed to the industry and made available to the news media and the general public. If you're curious about how your favorite airline ranks in the lost luggage complaint department, along with all other kinds of fun information on flight delays, incidents involving animals, etc., this is where you want to look. (It's some poor soul's job to compile that data each month, so you really ought to help make his life seem worthwhile and download it.)

If you want to impress your friends and make sure your missing luggage or travel horror story is documented for all time, or if you are just looking for additional ways to vent after your spouse has stopped listening to you and flipped on the TV, you can draft a formal letter of complaint to the Aviation Consumer Protection Division, U.S. Department of Transportation, 1200 New Jersey Ave, S.E., Washington, D.C. 20590, or use their handy web form on the site at airconsumer.ost.dot .gov/escomplaint/es.cfm. Be sure to include your flight information and a telephone number and e-mail address so they can get back to you if they have any questions. Go on. Try it. You'll feel much better!

If you are still not satisfied, you might consider posting to the ever-growing web community of disgruntled airline passengers and angry consumers at sites such as

- **My3Cents.com**: Consumer advice forum with an entire section dedicated to the airline industry.

- **Complaints.com**: Just what it sounds like, this searchable database will help you find others who have had similar experiences as yours. Group therapy only a mouse click away.

- **Yelp.com**: Have a blast complaining about airlines, hotels, limo companies, travel agencies—you can even weigh in your least favorite airports on here.

- **Untied.com**: Yes, the spelling is correct. This incredibly detailed site was started in 1996 after the president of United Airlines apparently refused to respond to a letter from Jeremy R. Cooperstock about the terrible service he received on his flight to Japan. Over a decade later, the site is still going strong, and has been featured in more than fifty publications worldwide, including *Forbes*, the *New York Times*, ABC News, etc. Business owners take note, Jeremy Cooperstock is one guy you do *not* want to piss off.

- **Amazon.com**: Can't really complain about an airline here, but you can go ahead and post a nice, friendly, glowing review for this book. Go on. It's guaranteed to make you feel better. ☺

Alternatively, you can try to figure out a solution to these difficult air travel industry problems yourself. Write to your congressman or congresswoman and propose an amendment to the procedures established by the Office of Aviation Enforcement and Proceedings Aviation Consumer Protection Division, and work endlessly to see its implementation. If you still can't get anyone to listen, you can start a campaign and run for local office, moving up through town, city, and state districts, spending your entire life savings and your golden years campaigning across the Midwest with your improved air transportation bill, until your political career comes to a screeching halt when word of your extramarital affair is leaked to the press and you wind up on the streets penniless and a mere shell of your former self. But man, will it be a ride.

The Only Safety Announcement
You Will Ever Need

I want to take a tiny break from the humor and indispensable advice here (come on, that thing about taping a picture of Clooney to your laptop was worth its weight in gold) to share something with you that I'm quite passionate about. Something I want to share with you and only you. Because you are someone who has been kind enough to invest your hard-earned money on this book, and I sincerely appreciate you doing so. And by doing so you and I have formed a special bond. (This is a very important concept I want you to keep in mind. I will explain why later on.)

But first, I have to tell you something. If you are listening to your iPod I'd like you to hit Pause just for a moment. (Just a moment, don't worry.) This is something that I firmly believe, and want you to as well, now that we are connected.

Are you ready? Here it is:

Never again will a plane have trouble taking off or landing.

Simple. I said it, and you read it.

Did you get it?

I'll say it again.

Never again will a plane have trouble taking off or landing.

Hmmm. I read that twice now, but I'm not really sure what you're talking about.

Okay, one last time.

Never again will a plane have trouble taking off or landing.

Okay, I'm done. Thank you. You can put your iPod back on.

CHAPTER 8

AIN'T NO THANG . . . FLYING WITHOUT FEAR

I ain't afraid of flyin'. I'm afraid of suddenly not flyin'.

If you are an average reader, what I wrote on the page preceding this chapter should have taken you seventeen seconds to read. Likely, you have no idea what I was talking about, and just thought it was another joke you didn't get, like the Aer Lingus one in chapter 7 you're probably still working on. (Seriously, don't ask your mom about that one.)

But what you read at the end of the last chapter was not a joke.

For seventeen seconds, I asked you to believe just what I do, that never again will a plane have trouble taking off or landing. For seventeen seconds you held that thought in your mind. And it has been scientifically proven that seventeen seconds is the exact amount of time it takes for the spark of a new idea to turn into a thought, which, when given enough focus and energy, will eventually become a belief. And I'm betting you're beginning to feel a bit better already, believing that thought.

Go back and read it again. Really believe what you're reading this time. Go on.

You might notice I didn't once use the term *plane crash*. Because to me, the word crash doesn't exist, other than referring to the sound a cymbal makes on a drum set.

Think about what I'm telling you. There never needs to be a plane that doesn't land as intended ever again. No malfunction, no hijacking, no engine failure, absolutely nothing. Every plane you ever board will take off safely and land safely at the destination printed on your ticket (unless your pilot opts to make a quick pit stop in Vegas to clear up a gambling debt). Just the same as every other plane in the world will take off and land safely. Imagine what the world will be like when you never have to worry that when you turn your off your cell phone, it will be for the last time.

It's not. You're going to land safely.

You never have to bug your children or your loved ones to remember to call you when they land.

You don't. They're going to land safely.

Just think about a world where we never hear of an airplane disaster ever again. Just think how amazing that world would be. Feel how amazing that world already is. Feel the relief, knowing you can fly wherever you want and never have to worry about it. If you are someone who already believes this, and perhaps has correctly guessed what I'm getting at here, then please make sure you're doing your part to help others, because this is something that's really important.

At the end of the book I've provided a little more information about the concept I've just presented to you. But for now, you don't have to understand everything. Just know one thing: You are going to land safely.

THERE'S NOTHING TO FEAR BUT FEAR ITSELF

If you have a fear of flying, you should immediately know that you are not alone. We face an unprecedented level of unease when flying these days. In fact, nearly 40 percent of the population admits to at least some level of anxiety when boarding a plane. (That's nearly one in two if you forgot your calculator.) And why shouldn't you be afraid? We've got security level threats in all colors of the rainbow, whackos trying to sneak all varieties of items on board in their shoes, incredibly stressful delays at every aspect of the air-travel process, and on top of all this, they've gone and taken away our one and only comfort food, the honey-roasted peanuts.

I'm sure you've heard it a thousand times. Flying is far safer than driving. And statistically, that's true. But you and I both know that when you're driving, you're in control. When you hop aboard a plane, you're trusting your entire existence to strangers. You just assume they are going to do their jobs up there. Navigating around unexpected weather patterns. Contacting air traffic control with radar updates. Monitoring the fuel gauges. Keeping an eye out for UFOs. Just as likely, they may be downing scotch and playing No Limit Texas Hold 'Em.

"That's crazy," you say. "Pilots haven't done that since the '70s."

Probably not, but how often do you arrive at your office and immediately get right down to work? I guarantee you spent at least the first hour forwarding joke emails and scouring the web for any new videos of cats that can surf or fat kids stuffing french fries in their mouths. And if you had permission from your boss to lock your door, carry a gun, and not speak to anyone until your shift is over, would you *really* spend every waking moment hard at work?

Oh, but I jest. Truth is, the folks in charge of driving the plane are highly trained professionals with years of experience whose primary focus is your safety. In fact, you could learn a thing or two from commercial airline pilots. Rarely will you find them yammering on the cell phone, changing the radio station, eating a sandwich and yelling at the kids in the back seat while trying to merge into lanes of traffic. And due to updated FAA regulations, pilots are now only allowed to bring one small bottle of scotch on board. So you're in good hands.

But knowing you're in good hands doesn't always equate with peace of mind, especially when you're sailing through turbulence so bad it knocks the glasses off your head and makes you pee your pants. If you *truly* want to overcome your fear of flying, read this chapter carefully. The power to calm your fears is in your mind, and always has been. If you just want the extra attention and want everyone to feel bad for you, feel free to skip ahead.

SOMETIMES THEY COME, SOMETIMES THEY DON'T

If you've ever traveled through Italy, you've probably heard someone offer the phrase "Sometimes they come, sometimes they don't" as the simple explanation to their country's lack of modern transportation. Buses, trains, and taxis all seem to operate on their own little Old World Italian time clocks. This may be considered charming to some. Yet on my first flight on Air Italia, I found myself praying their airplanes don't operate by a similar motto, "Sometimes they land, sometimes they don't."

I never had a fear of flying when I was younger. I loved the family trips we took, and I even considered becoming a pilot when I grew up.[34] I recall sailing through thunderstorms and turbulence so bad you couldn't even hold on to a drink or deck of cards, and it didn't bother me in the least. I have been on a plane that lost an engine, and I barely woke up from my nap long enough to register we had been circling

---

34.   Well, truthfully, the ship I wanted to pilot was the Black Lion, as commander of the Voltron force, to save the planet Arus from the evil clutches of Haggar the witch while restoring peace throughout the galaxy. Unfortunately, they didn't have that job listing in our high school guidance counselor's office, so I ended up delivering pizza after school. But I've yet to give up on the dream.

over the ocean for an hour, jettisoning fuel on some unsuspecting surfers before returning to the airport on three remaining engines. But in the fall of 2005, all of that changed. On an early morning Air Italia flight returning from Europe, I was jolted awake by the sound of a sudden bang from the left wing. Although there was no noticeable loss of altitude or airspeed, I thought we were going down for sure. I had stayed awake the entire night before at the airport (I had run out of money and couldn't afford a hotel room), and my sleep-deprived mind failed to register anything other than the fact that a loud noise came from somewhere a loud noise shouldn't come from. Unfortunately, or perhaps fortunately, I didn't understand a word the Italian pilot was saying over the intercom, and my panic soon reached unprecedented levels.

I later learned the sound I heard might have simply been a compressor stalling (*compressore in stallo*), a somewhat common occurrence in older aircraft due to uneven airflow through the engine. Or we could've hit a large, lazy Italian bird (*ucello pigro*). Or it could've even been my imagination (*insano*). In fact, this was probably the most logical explanation, as I don't recall any other passengers looking up from their cannoli and espressos for even a brief moment. Or maybe they all knew something I didn't, which is that Air Italia airplanes are just noisy as f-ck.

Regardless, the next couple of years of flying proved to be more than a little nerve-wracking. My heartbeat shot through the roof on every takeoff and landing, and every strange sound in between. Sleep never came. Throughout each flight I was fully prepared to run up front and land the plane at the slightest indication that the pilot and entire flight staff had suddenly fallen unconscious, relying on the piloting expertise I had gained from watching the *Airplane* and *Airplane II* movies.

Why the long, anticlimactic narrative to start the chapter? Because I'm fairly certain I'm not alone in the fear of flying, and if I do nothing else on this earth, I hope to use my ridiculous experiences to help others.

My Phobia Has Phobias

Why is the fear of flying so prevalent? For many, the experience of flying is a combination of many fears, all tied up in one nice convenient package. Along with Aerophobia or Aviatophobia, "the basic fear of flying"; you've got Acrophobia, "fear of heights"; Aeroacrophobia, "fear of open high places"; Aeronausiphobia, "fear of vomiting due to airsickness"; Arachibutyrophobia, "fear of peanut butter sticking to the roof of the mouth" (much more common now that you can't carry a bottle of water with you through security); Anglophobia, "fear of England or English culture" (prevalent on British Airways flights); Anuptaphobia, "fear of dying single"; Astraphobia, "fear of thunder and lightning"; Autodysomophobia, "fear of people with vile odors"; and Autophobia, "fear of being alone." And that's only the letter A.

Some overachievers go one step further, the fear of fear. Also known as Anticipatory Anxiety, many sufferers begin to exhibit signs of panic attacks months prior to a flight. Do yourself a favor. Do not simply tell yourself not to worry, and hope that the condition will go away. This will not work. Again, if the world of professional wrestling[35] has taught us anything, it's that you need to face your fears head on. You'll feel much better the next time you fly.

---

35.   If you weren't aware, the World Wrestling Federation changed its name to World Wrestling Entertainment in 2000, when they were sued by the environmental organization World Wide Fund for Nature. As lame as that sounds, the WWF obliged, and changed its name and initials to WWE, using the clever slogan "Get the 'F' Out." Why is this important? It just is.

WHAT THE F#%@ WAS THAT NOISE? A QUICK GUIDE TO COMMON AIRCRAFT NOISES THAT DON'T INDICATE IMMEDIATE DEATH

While experts vary in their approach to overcoming the fear of flying, they all do agree on one basic fundamental: Knowledge is power. You don't need further stress and undue anxiety worrying about strange aircraft noises and things that go bump in the flight.

In my own case, had I understood what the noise was that I heard on my rickety little Air Italia airplane (or had I known Italian), my airborne anxiety would never have spiraled out of control. If you really want to prepare for your next flight, visit some of the sites listed at the end of this section, where you can play actual sound clips of many common aircraft noises. You may find you'll be a lot more relaxed knowing that what you're hearing is nothing but the normal operation of the airplane. Or you may have a panic attack at your computer. (But isn't that better than having one while flying?) And yes, there will be a quiz later.

- **Thumping sound**: Landing gear being retracted.

- **A sound like a drill or a crazy monkey**: Flaps and spoilers retracting.

- **Slamming sound**: Cargo or luggage that was not properly secured may have shifted on takeoff. Or a little kid slamming his tray and throwing a tantrum.

- **A sound like the airplane lost power**: Air conditioning shifting or engines reducing speed. Perfectly normal.

- **Ticking or clicking**: Normal operation of landing flaps.

- **Enormous bang**: Pilot fell asleep with his foot on the gas pedal and you have surpassed the speed of sound, resulting in a sonic boom.

- **A small hissing sound, followed by a smell like foul baloney**: No cause for alarm. The person next to you is releasing gas.

SOME COMMON ADDITIONAL CAUSES FOR CONCERN, WHICH ARE REALLY NOT CAUSES FOR CONCERN

- **Yah, um, there's the end of the runway . . . so why are we still on the ground?** Airplane engines are often run far below capacity to preserve engine life. While it may seem as though you're not going anywhere near fast enough to get off the ground, this is usually the pilot scaling back on the engines and using a little more runway for a longer takeoff. And don't worry, there is always the option to push the throttle and "gun it" at the last minute if needed. Unless you notice that you are already in the water (in which case you may want to proceed directly to the end of this chapter for island survival tips).

- **Plane suddenly tipping from side to side during takeoff.** The pilot is simply getting the feel of the aircraft. It may surprise you to know that just like a female's breasts, it is quite common for one wing of the airplane to be heavier than the other, due to varying levels of fuel stored in the tanks located in the wings. Hee, hee. Tanks.

- **We're climbing, but it feels like the engines just shut off.** About thirty seconds after takeoff, engine thrust is often reduced to comply with airport noise restrictions. This sudden change may feel like the plane is about to fall back toward the ground. It's not. You may also experience a sudden lightheadedness. Just imagine you're in a giant elevator about to level off on the top floor (unless you have a fear of elevators).

- **Everything just got *really* quiet.** The pilot is simply reducing engine power, or you may have entered a time warp and are traveling back in time. To determine which one it is, look out the window and see if you notice any dinosaurs. Additionally, they may be filming a movie on your flight, and someone is about to say an important line.

■ **Crazy banking or turning for no reason.** You ended up on a flight with an ex-military pilot trying to relive some of his glory days. Relax. The missiles on commercial airplanes are all disabled. The worst they can do is bomb the villages below with bags of stale pretzels.

Stop! Before proceeding with the next section, you must complete the following quiz:

Pop Quiz: Airplanes and Flying

Fourth-grade Science
Professor Michaels

1. Can a wing snap off a plane due to turbulence?

   a. Yes.

   b. No

   c. Only if global warming predictions come true, and you encounter a thunderstorm the size of Russia

2. How much would you have to bend a wing in order to snap it off a plane?

   a. Five feet

   b. Ten feet

   c. A whole lot

3. How much does a plane move up or down during moderate turbulence?

   a. Fifty to one hundred feet

    b. Ten to fifteen feet

    c. Sometimes only a few inches

4. In the history of air travel, how many planes have fallen out of the sky from normal turbulence?

    a. Too many to count

    b. Fewer than one hundred

    c. Zero.

5. Are pilots afraid of turbulence?

    a. Yes.

    b. No.

    c. Only unexpected turbulence, which could knock their poker chips all over the cockpit.

Okay, class, let's see how you did. In case you didn't see it coming, the correct answer to every question is c. Let's review!

THE WIND BENEATH MY WINGS

The wings on an airplane are designed to withstand pretty much anything nature throws at them. And in fact, the term *wings* is a little misleading, since on many aircraft the "wings" are really a solid piece of construction that passes through the fuselage (main body of the plane). What may to you look like a wing about to break in half is really just the normal flex of the design. If the material didn't bend, wings would snap off like a piece of glass.

If you want to see an example of the severe pressure wings are built to withstand, google "Wing Stress Test of a Boeing 777," and check out the very cool video clip anywhere fine videos are shown. Boeing actually destroyed an entire airplane to make sure the company's engineers remembered to carry all the ones and zeros when they were designing their new 777. As predicted, the wings withstood forces greater than 150 percent of the maximum forces they should ever encounter in flight, until they finally snapped with a big, resounding bang at 154 percent, and over twenty-four feet of deflection from their standard horizontal position.[36]

Unless a plane was to travel at a speed far, far greater than normal, there is simply no way to generate enough force, or what is referred to as lift, to bend the wings enough to damage them. Even if you encounter an alien spaceship that locks on to your plane with a tractor beam and drags you across the galaxy at ten times the speed of light, the wings will remain attached to your airplane as there is no atmospheric pressure in the vast recess of space to rip them off. Of course, whether or not they will withstand reentry forces depends on the atmospheric conditions of the planet where you land. Luckily, most aliens take this into consideration when they abduct you. And if you ask, airlines will generally refund the price of your plane ticket if you do happen to be abducted.

Okay. So are we done with wings?

Let's move on.

TURBULENCE, AND OTHER ANNOYING THINGS THAT BEGIN WITH THE LETTER T

While doing research for this chapter, I came across an unfathomable amount of posts on Internet chat boards from people all around the world who share the fear of flying. Old, young, seasoned jetsetters,

---

36. No matter how may protractors and scientific calculators were lying around that day, it was impossible to determine precisely how much money was won as a result of side bets between the hordes of engineers watching the test in what was their single greatest day of work. No doubt, those who lost are waiting patiently for double or nothing odds on Boeing's 787, whose wings are rumored to be so strong they can bend far enough to touch each other above the fuselage. Bring it.

inexperienced travelers, and those who are so scared to fly they would
rather deal with the horror of packing their screaming kids into a minivan and spending a week driving across the entire country than set one
foot inside an airplane.

Many of these posts seemed to center around one thing:
turbulence.

*I am afraid of turbulence, especially when it's sudden and unex-
pected. In particular, I don't like when the plane drops. When I was a
child I used to enjoy it. I thought it was fun, like a roller coaster ride.
Now I can't barely let go of the armrest long enough to reach for the
barf bag.*

—Anonymous flyer

OMG. I hate turbulence. It is so not fun. LOL.

—Anonymous female teenager

*I hate flying. I hate turbulence. I hate being trapped in a narrow,
metal tube. The only way I can tolerate it is to knock myself out
with an Ambien. But I love to travel. Forward this message to 50
friends in the next two minutes, and the phone will ring in one hour
with good news. (THIS REALLY WORKS!) If you don't forward
this to at least 20 friends, you will die within an hour.*

—Anonymous idiot

After frantically trying to come up with fifty friends to forward
that to who are now never going to speak to me again, these posts got
me thinking: a) how did so many people develop a fear of turbulence?
and b) who's paying for all this storage space on the Internet?

It seems the older we get, the more we fear things that begin with
the letter *T*: turbulence, taxes, talking in front of crowds, turning forty,

Thanksgiving with the in-laws, Tom Cruise coming on your talk show and jumping on your couch. It's inevitable.

Nobody likes to be bounced and jostled in his seat like a human cat toy, but it's a part of flying, and not something to fear. If nothing else, turbulence is a reminder that there is air all around you keeping the plane aloft. Yet most don't view it this way.

Unfortunately, there's not much you can do to avoid turbulence, except down another Xanax and keep reading. And remember, the more knowledge you have about what's happening, the less likely you are to pee your pants, which is always a good goal.

Turbulence occurs when an aircraft flies through masses of air moving in different directions, which can be a result of the jet stream, passing warm or cold fronts, air passing over mountains, air displaced in the wake of other aircraft (damn UFOs again), or thunderstorms.

Most turbulence you encounter is of the standard variety, what pilots often refer to as "chop." You can feel an airplane moving as little as a few inches up or down when it encounters chop. Remember, you are traveling at speeds of more than 500 mph, so everything is magnified. Sort of like hitting a bump on the pavement in a car. If you drive over a tiny bump while backing out of your driveway, you'll probably never even notice. Hit the same bump going 90 mph down the freeway, and you'll spill your coffee all over you. But neither is going to tear apart your car (unless you drive a Prius).

Chances are, the bumps and shakes that have you gripping your rosary beads are so minor that the pilots and flight attendants will barely remember them by the time you land. Remember, planes can and do routinely fly through hurricanes, and that makes for some good shaking.

How Do You Spell Overcoming Airborne Anxiety? J-E-L-L-O.

Bill Cosby, anyone? No? Too young? Well, if you're still worried about your plane falling out of the sky, America's most famous dessert is once again coming to your rescue. As suggested by the SOAR Conquer Fear of Flying Course (and others who enjoy food analogies to get their point across), try to visualize your plane as being a piece of fruit trapped in a giant bowl of Jell-O. The Jell-O represents the air within the earth's atmosphere. (It doesn't matter the flavor, but Berry Blue seems appropriate.) Shake the Jell-O all you want, the fruit is not going to drop to the bottom of the bowl. The folks at SOAR even go so far as to suggest building a model airplane and sticking it inside a bowl of Jell-O. If this helps, I say go for it. Just remember to remove the airplane before you serve desert.

I would also suggest hiring a professional female Jell-O wrestler (or two) to come to your house to shake the bowl for you. Just to help drive the point home.

CLEAR AIR TURBULENCE: A CHIROPRACTOR'S DREAM

In a few instances, turbulence can be worrisome for pilots. One type is clear air turbulence. As you might imagine, clear air turbulence often occurs without a cloud in the sky. This is sometimes erroneously referred to as hitting an "air pocket," a term coined by a reporter during World War I. Really, there is no such thing as a pocket of air. This would be the same as describing a pocket of water in the ocean, where a ship could suddenly fall to the ocean floor. They don't exist (except in Bikini Bottom on *SpongeBob Squarepants* and select episodes of *The Snorks*.) But if it helps you to picture it, you can call it an air pocket.

When flying through clear air turbulence, the pilot's fear still isn't that the plane is going to fall out of the sky, but that passengers in the cabin may be injured by a sudden loss of altitude, causing potential head, neck, and back injuries. Precisely why they ask that you keep your seatbelt on at all times.

Another type of turbulence that pilots watch out for is called "wind shear." This is a rapid change in direction of air currents, often as a result of thunderstorms or unusually hot temperatures. Wind shear can be potentially dangerous if it occurs close to the ground and affects the flight path of an aircraft flying at slow speeds. But airports monitor wind shear closely, and pilots simply avoid flying anywhere near thunderstorms. So don't be all angry when your flight is delayed due to bad weather; it's people looking out for your safety. (That, and the baggage guys don't like to work in the rain.)

OVERCOME YOUR FEAR OF FLYING IN FIVE MINUTES OR LESS

If all of this Knowledge is Power crap is doing nothing to keep your palms from sweating and your heart from pounding its way out of your chest cavity as the plane lurches and jostles its way about the sky, don't worry. We've got a few more tricks up our sleeve.

If you happen to be bouncing along inside a plane right now, look around you.[37] What do you see? Actually, in the interest of time, I'll just tell you what you see: scared adults and happy kids.

---

37. If you're at home or in the bookstore reading this, just bounce up and down in your chair to simulate some light chop.

Do You Care?

Don't care about any of this? Do you only want to fly through blue skies as smooth as a baby's butt? Check out Turbulenceforecast. com, where you can assess predicted turbulence levels across the globe prior to flying. Turbulenceforcast.com pulls maps and data from the National Oceanic and Atmospheric Administration (NOAA), and other weather sites around the world. Ratings range from Smooth Ride to Severe, and indicate the region and altitude turbulence is likely to be experienced. You can even impress your friends by adding a cool turbulence index to your blog or Facebook page, or access a mobile version at the airport on your BlackBerry or iPod touch at m.turbulenceforecast. com. If you're headed on a cruise, be sure to check out the section on predicted wave heights before you hit the buffet.

When is the last time you saw a kid look up from his video game because the plane started shaking? Kids aren't afraid of flying. The bumpier, the better. But as you start to mature, the voices in the back of your head grow a little louder. *This is your fifth flight this month Kevin. Don't you think you're pushing your odds buddy?*

Thankfully, there are ways to ease the pain and rewind our brains back to their blissful, childlike state. The first, and most obvious, is to have a little drinky drink. There is no shame in downing a few shots or a couple of glasses of wine as soon as you get on board, after which you will undoubtedly revert to acting like a child. But, alas, the relief is only temporary.

For true, lasting change in overcoming your flying fears, you're gonna need a little therapy.

Oh, don't be scared. Just because therapy is another *T* word doesn't mean you should fear it or dread it. Nor does it require a visit to an intimidating psychologist's office, or lying on a couch as a creepy guy with glasses swings a watch in front of your face and tells you you are growing sleepy while eyeing the top button on your blouse or the zipper on your trousers. That's old-school therapy. And while that approach might work, I'm talking about starting with nothing more than a little positive thinking and a little self-inflicted pain. Sounds like more fun, doesn't it?

First, it may come as a shock to you, but I do not have a PhD in psychology. I know, I know. I come off as an incredible intellectual, with complete comprehension of the human condition, but truth be told, I'm just a guy who really enjoys watching other people doing stupid things and then writing about it. However, as I mentioned at the beginning of this chapter, I was able to cure my own fear of flying and I feel a responsibility to at least try to cure yours. Here's how.

FIVE STEPS TO FLYING FREEDOM

Step 1: Rationalization

I simply told myself that people fly every day, and that some even fly for a living. And I looked at the ten-year-old sitting next to me, flying all by himself, with his little neatly printed nametag on his chest. I told myself, *If he can do it, so can I.* This worked surprisingly well—until the bumps hit.

Step 2: Distraction

This is also known as "lying to yourself." This involved listening to loud music with my headphones, engaging my row mates in conversation, or focusing intently on in-flight movies I would otherwise completely ignore. As you likely well know, this only works so long as the plane is flying smoothly. At the first sign of a bump, you'll find you've actually been doing more harm than good. Because by avoiding your fear, you've given your anxiety an open door to take over.

Step 3: Safety in Numbers

When I travel with a companion or in a group, I find I'm generally relaxed. Maybe this is because I don't want to look like a crybaby in front of my friends. This confidence is magically absent when I'm traveling alone. And, of course, almost exclusively, when I'm traveling alone is when the big turbulence hits.

Step 4: Knowledge Is Power

I've already presented the idea of Knowledge is Power to you. Knowing what was going on with the airplane *greatly* enhanced my ability to cope. But, on occasion, I could feel that irrational fear creeping back into my mind . . .

Step 5: Slapping Yourself in the Face

This one finally did it.

"Surely, you can't be serious," you ask.

I am. (And stop calling me "Shirley.")

Using some form of pain (or any sudden, unexpected stimulus) to interrupt an irrational thought process is by no means a new concept. Think back to when you were a kid. If you were afraid of the dark or worried about monsters under the bed, and you had an older brother around to smack you upside the head or give you a noogie anytime he felt you were acting like a baby, you likely grew out of your fears very quickly. If you were an only child, or didn't have an older figure there to "smack some sense into you," I'm willing to bet you still sleep with a nightlight.

It may seem crude and barbaric, but it does work. And here's why. Everything you experience in life is recorded as energy impulses within the brain, which are also referred to as "neural associations." Sort of like a computer writing data to hard drive, if you will. The more times the data is written, the stronger the neural association. What your older brother was doing when he smacked you around was interrupting your thought process and inhibiting your mind from effectively developing an association linking your bedroom with a fear of the dark or monsters. Of course, no doubt your brother simply wanted to kick the crap out of you. But the result was the same.

When it comes to the fear of flying, it's that much harder to erase these neural associations causing your anxiety because they've likely been imprinted in your brain for years. If you think back to your very first flight, you were probably one of those kids you see now, cheering as the plane hits another rough bump. Somewhere along the way you were presented with outside information that solidified itself in your brain until all you now know about flying is associated with this newer information. Maybe you had an experience when you hit some particularly scary turbulence during a flight, or your plane suddenly dropped in altitude (which you now simply recognize as clear air turbulence), and it replays itself in your mind every time you fly. Or maybe, you simply watch the evening news, where the media does a real nice job at scaring the bejeezus out of us. Either way, the only way to fully cure your fear is to begin erasing these associations and replacing them with new ones.

There are many ways to accomplish this: hypnosis, autosuggestion, meditation—they all work. Some psychologists might even have you address your fears as if they are real people, and get angry at them.

Pretend they are your mother. Who does she think she is, butting in and trying to run your life?

But if you want quick and effective relief, slap yourself in the face as soon as you feel that fear start to creep in. Or have someone next to you do it. If I happen to be on your flight, I'll be more than happy to smack you—anything to help a fellow passenger.

If you want a more civilized approach, keep a thick elastic band around your wrist when you fly, as suggested by Dr. Duane Brown in *Flying Without Fear.* When you begin to feel that irrational fear creeping into your mind, remove the elastic and snap yourself in the palm of your hand sharply to interrupt your thought process, and tell yourself to simply stop thinking these destructive thoughts. Then make sure to replace them with positive thoughts about flying. Don't just mumble to yourself that flying is safe. Focus on overcoming your fears with as much intensity as you can, as the subconscious mind will respond to your emotions. You may want to chant a little mantra or poem. You know the type: "Every day, in every way, I'm getting better and better." Or practice creating some of your own. Get your whole row to chant along with you.

In time, you will learn to control your mind, and control your fears. The human brain is a complex and wonderful organ, but many times it simply gets the better of us. If your fear of flying is truly to the point where it incapacitates you, I would encourage you to take a fear-of-flying course, several of which are listed under "Additional Resources" in this chapter. There are even flight simulators where you can practice your techniques, without ever having to step foot on a plane. There is really no need to keep yourself from experiencing the world and all it has to offer.

Psych 101: Anatomy of a Panic Attack

A panic attack is the body's way of preparing itself for danger. You may have heard the term "fight or flight," and recognize the symptoms of shortness of breath, heart beating wildly, sweaty palms, etc. All of these are the result of the *mind* telling the *body* there is imminent danger, and the body is simply preparing to deal.

Your heartbeat increases because the brain is hell-bent on pumping more blood to the areas of the body where it thinks it will be needed, such as the legs, arms, and other large, action-oriented muscles. You may also notice your fingers and toes growing numb, or a tingling sensation in your hands and feet, as the blood flows away from the outermost parts of the body. This is the body's way of further protecting itself, and to keep you from bleeding to death in the event you are gravely injured. (If you are a male, you may also recognize this as shrinkage, or the reason why your date never returned your call.)

Your breathing will also become highly accelerated, as the body attempts to push as much oxygen as possible throughout the body. This can result in feelings of dizziness or light-headedness as the heavy breathing will decrease blood going to the head. You will also begin to sweat profusely, which is the body's internal cooling system ensuring that you do not overheat while in action, as well as making the skin into a slippery surface, harder for a predator to grab.

And finally, you may feel like you're losing your mind as you find yourself unable to concentrate on a simple task or even remember your own name. This is simply your mind preparing itself to focus all of its attention on the immediate danger. It shuts off any thought process it deems unnecessary. As you are accustomed to accessing this information whenever you need it, you begin to feel as though you are "going crazy." Nothing could be further from the truth. You're already crazy.

ADDITIONAL RESOURCES

Many of these sites offer complete courses or CDs or DVDs you can purchase. You can also find a large number of videos on YouTube depicting normal aircraft noises you can use to practice desensitizing yourself to flying, as well as hundreds of tips and tricks to overcome anxiety. YouTube is also home to an astounding array of scenes involving girls in bikinis washing cars. Watching a few hundred of these nightly will surely calm your nerves.

- Fearlessflight.com
- Flyingwithoutfear.com
- Fromthecockpit.com
- Fearofflyinghelp.com
- Fearofflying.com
- Gogetterjetsetter.com

SOME ADDITIONAL USELESS RESOURCES

- *Fear of Flying*, CD by R&B artist Mya—(includes "Case of the Ex (Whatcha Gonna Do)" and "Lie Detector (featuring 'Beenie Man').
- *Fear of Flying* by Erica Jong, the steamy, controversial, 1970s novel about female sexuality.

WAIT! DON'T GO! UH, WHAT IF *ALL* THE ENGINES GO OUT AT THE SAME TIME? WHAT IF WE RUN OUT OF FUEL?

Even if all the engines happen to fail at the same time, you're still not going to fall out of the sky. Even the heaviest of jumbo jets have a glide ratio of about 15:1, meaning that for every one mile of altitude a plane can glide for fifteen miles. An airplane at a cruising altitude of thirty thousand feet is able to glide for approximately eighty miles, or roughly thirty minutes. In fact, when descending, a common practice is to run the engines at what is known as idle thrust, where the engine is running but producing no forward momentum, in effect, gliding. If the engines go out, all the pilot has to do is find a nearby airport, and glide on in. And airplanes are even equipped with a little button they can hit to plot a course to the nearest airport. (Sort of like the button on your GPS you can hit to find the nearest Burger King.) Granted, they only get one shot at the landing, and they may shut your movie off to conserve power. But you can probably get the $5 for the headphones refunded.

Running out of fuel can also be a major concern for many passengers, although it need not be. Perhaps you've been on a plane that the pilot decided to taxi back to the gate because at the last minute he decided to put a little more gas in the tank. You might've shifted uncomfortably in your seat, wondering just what might've happened had the pilot not taken the time to glance at the gas gauge. In most cases, nothing. This is just the pilot planning for the possibility of a slightly modified flight plan. A commercial aircraft is required to have enough fuel on board to reach its destination, make a missed approach, fly to an alternate landing, hold for thirty minutes, and still land with 10 percent of fuel in its tanks. If only your husband were that prepared.

Additionally, any time there is even a minor incident involving any aircraft, it is fully investigated by the aviation division of the National Transportation Safety Board, and each instance is a chance to learn what can be done better to enhance passenger safety in the future. In contrast, when it comes to enhancing passenger safety when driving a car, there is really no new information. Get off the damn cell phone.

And always remember, there is one person far more concerned than you that your plane will arrive safely on the ground: the pilot. Getting another pilot job after wrecking a $150 million jet can be very difficult, and unlike other professions, there is little else an ex-pilot can do.

Have you ever seen an ex-pilot fixing the copier in your office, or packing groceries in your local supermarket? No. These alpha individuals only understand one thing: how to operate six miles up in the sky while racing across the atmosphere at the speed of sound. Like a world champion prizefighter or Carrot Top, pilots thrive on the adrenaline rush their occupation gives them. Rest assured, the very last thing they want to do is be fired for missing a runway. Especially since they'll never hear the end of it from the guys at the airport bar.

A FEW MORE FACTS TO EASE THE MIND

- Pilots are not allowed to fly within twenty miles of a thunderstorm, and it is illegal for pilots to fly through thunderstorms.
- If lightning hits an aircraft you will be perfectly safe. The lightning simply passes through the plane since it's not connected to the ground. (Although you may come off the plane with temporary superpowers.)
- To avoid even the chance of a head-on collision, eastbound flights fly at odd altitudes, and westbound flights fly at even altitudes, putting a good thousand feet between them. Of course, this

doesn't take into account UFOs, which may not be accustomed to our earthly units of measure. But this is precisely why airplanes have radars, and they make sure to squeegee the front windows every time they fill up the gas tank.

Now, ideally your mind is more at ease, and you are in the perfect state to contemplate the next section. Hope you remembered to pack your swimsuit!

CHAPTER 9

IN THE EVENT OF A WATER LANDING

You land a million planes safely, then you have one little mid-air and you
never hear the end of it. —Air traffic controller in *Pushing Tin*

SURVIVOR SEASON 172: ~~AFRICA, THE OUT-BACK, AMAZON.COM~~, UH . . . WHERE ARE WE EXACTLY?

While no one ever plans on landing anywhere except the location
printed on your ticket, occasionally a pilot will find himself a little lost
in the clouds and refuse to ask for directions (recall that the majority of
airline pilots are male), and you may find the oxygen masks tumbling
out of the ceiling as you touch down in a remote jungle somewhere in
the Pacific.

Try not to panic. Look to the left of you. Look to the right.[38] The
real fear isn't crashing. The real fear is these people just might become
your family for the next few seasons of a reality TV show.

If you've ever wondered why you should be nice to everyone you
meet, this is why. It has nothing to do with adhering to some golden
rule. It's for your own protection. Imagine having to live with an entire
planeload of passengers your crying baby kept awake, or being sent

---

38. Unless you're sitting on a window seat, in which case just look the opposite direction from
the window, pause for effect, then turn and look the same way again.

into the jungle to search for food with the person you vomited on after turning in your entire booklet of free-drink coupons. There is a real good chance your name is going to pop up repeatedly when the others are trying to decide who's for dinner.

But before you cancel your next flight and swear off air travel for the rest of your life, consider some benefits of remote island living:

- Easy to deplane through gaping hole in hull.
- Won't have to wait in long lines in baggage claim to retrieve your luggage.
- You will most likely receive free lifetime passes to the Admiral's Club in exchange for the minor inconvenience upon your return to society.
- Extended paid vacation. Most companies will not dock your pay if you are stranded on a deserted island. Tom Hanks was absent from his job at FedEx for four years after being stuck on the island in *Cast Away*, and they still offered him the good shifts when he returned. They even paid his therapy bills. (Unfortunately, his position of husband didn't remain open quite so long, as Helen Hunt moved in with the new guy pretty much right away. Hey, you can't win them all.)

And be sure to check with your airline about getting credited for the extra frequent flyer miles to whatever island you eventually landed on. The miles could really add up.

Additionally, there are a great many books written on surviving on a deserted island. While I find this somewhat odd (and a little creepy), you can certainly benefit from the trial and error of others. Since there is way too much information for you to ever remember, the best way to prepare yourself is to simply download a few audio books onto your iPod. Be sure to put them on a playlist marked "For Island Survival."

Then it's there should you ever need it. (Just make certain to keep your iPod fully charged. Apple stores are tough to locate in the jungle.)

If you have a video iPod, you may also want to go ahead and download a few episodes of *Survivor* or *Gilligan's Island*, just in case you come across any useful tips. (While you might think it would be appropriate, I wouldn't recommend downloading any episodes of *Lost*. In the time it will take you to decipher a single plot you could have shot and killed your first meal; stockpiled a lifetime supply of coconuts; or possibly even erected an entire village with paved roads, a modern school system, and cozy cafés with WiFi and open mic nights run by the local natives.)

WE DIDN'T START THE FIRE (BUT WE SHOULD HAVE)

If it begins to look like you're going to be spending a lot more time than you originally planned in your new island home (which was none), the first thing you're going to want to do is build a fire. Fire is key for keeping warm, preparing food, warding off dinosaurs, sending smoke signals to alert rescue planes, and when your flashlight batteries run out, it will be your only source of light at night. Some will argue that the first thing you need to do is find shelter, but anyone can tape together some leaves or tie some sweatshirts between a couple of palm trees and make a tent. The ones who can make fire . . . well, they shall rule the kingdom.

Fire is also a necessary element for singing camp songs, which is key to maintaining the morale of your fellow passengers. Have you ever seen a group of campers singing around a pile of wet sweatshirts?

As you wander around hunting for sticks to rub together, you may quickly discover that living without electricity sucks, and also that Billy

Joel lies a lot in his songs. There is no eternal fire that's been always burning since the world's been turning from which you can light your torch and work on your Sudokus while you await rescue. And while Billy Joel may be able to afford to hire someone to build a fire for him, you may not be so fortunate.

Also, you may quickly discover just how difficult a task starting a fire can prove to be. Best to get started right away.

THE COKE CAN AND THE CHOCOLATE BAR

Ideally, you've landed on your new island home with a large group of smokers. Not only will their need to buy cigarettes drive them to astounding lengths in order to figure out a way to get you all off the island quickly, they'll also likely have a match or two on them. Make sure they store the matches in some type of waterproof bag, lest someone pushes them into the water in a game of chicken and your only hope at survival goes up in flames . . . er . . . water.

If you don't have matches, a lighter, or any other type of fire-making device, it's time to get creative. And honestly, you've got nothing but time, so you might as well try as many methods as you can.

Begin rubbing the bottom of the Coke can (Pepsi will do) with your chocolate bar until you get it as shiny as possible, or until you eat the candy bar out of starvation. If you don't have a chocolate bar, toothpaste will also work as a polishing agent, but good luck finding any on board with the new 3-1-1 carry-on rules. (For the sake of argument, we'll also assume that for some reason the bathroom mirrors, rearview mirrors, magnifying glasses, eyeglasses, and all the shiny objects were missing from your airplane, and this one can of Coke is your only chance at survival.)

Ask a volunteer to stand next to you, then point the bottom of the can toward his face. If it burns his eyes out, it's shiny enough. If not, keep polishing. If you are alone on the island, do not point the can at your own eyes. You will need them later. (Why Coca-Cola doesn't just save the island folks a lot of work and make the bottoms of their cans shiny to begin with is beyond me.)

After you've shined your can, hold it out about an inch from a dry leaf, or whatever else you can find for tinder, and angle it so the bottom reflects the sun directly onto the leaf. A small smoldering should start momentarily. Your tinder should be balled up loosely to allow plenty of airflow. Blow on it slowly until you have a roaring blaze. Don't forget to have plenty of pretzel bags or Sudoku puzzle books available to add once the fire really starts cooking.[39]

Also, be sure not to start your fire on the edge of the woods, or you may simply end up burning the entire island to the ground. Which would be tragic, yet may show up on a satellite picture, and therefore potentially increase your chances of being rescued. Your call.

BALLOON AND A CONDOM

Assuming you have a box of condoms, a bag of party balloons, or a supply of Ziplock bags with you on the island, you can try this fire-lighting

---

39.   Alas, if all other paper products have blown off your island, and all that remains is this book, go on and use it to fuel your blaze. Like the Giving Tree, who gave every part of itself throughout its life until it was nothing left but a stump for others to sit on, I am prepared to make the ultimate sacrifice for your well-being. Go forth and burn brightly, little book. Burn brightly. (Be sure to avoid the toxic fumes that will be released from the cover as it burns.) I will also be more than happy to replace it for you on your return to the mainland, free of charge, providing you send me proof you were stranded on an island. Pictures with you alongside some island natives in ragged clothing and a four-month growth of beard should suffice. Or a coconut.

trick. Fill your condom, balloon, or baggie with enough water to fill it but not distort its shape, then tie off the end. Squeeze the bag so the sunlight passing through forms a sharp circle of light, which you can then direct onto your tinder.

Try to avoid squeezing too hard in case the balloon, bag, or condom breaks. Also try to avoid using a used condom. Not only is it gross, it's difficult to focus a beam of light through any fluid other than water. If you've only got one condom left and must decide between having safe sex or creating a fire that could possibly save your life, well, good luck to you sir.

IS THAT A GUN IN YOUR POCKET?

If you've got access to the airplane's cockpit, you should be able to find at least one gun lying around. Remove one of the bullets from its cartridge, then pour half of the powder onto your tinder. Place the half-empty cartridge back in the gun (without the bullet), then fire it at the tinder. Make sure to set up your tinder in an enclosed area or at the base of a tree, as the blast from the gun will likely blow the tinder away, and extinguish the very same flame you worked so hard to create. As with the condom conundrum, if there is only one bullet remaining and you have the choice between starting a fire or killing the evil creature about to attack your camp, well, again I say good luck to you sir.

A FEW MORE FIRE-STARTING METHODS

- Wait for someone to spontaneously combust. (It's always the quiet ones.)

- Ask if anyone in your group has fire-starting superpowers. Many times stressful situations (such as landing on a deserted island) can alter the chemical makeup of a human and create special powers without them ever realizing it, like the X-Men. Be sure to check with everyone twice. It's not uncommon for someone to mistake indigestion for the ability to breathe fire.

- Anger a Latina. (This shouldn't be too difficult.) Many times you can see the smoke coming from her eyes when she is pissed. Try to hold a dry leaf as close to her head as possible.[40]

---

40. I feel like I might get in trouble with this one too, so I'll just go ahead and apologize now to the entire Latin female population. But remember, this is important information that could save someone's life.

CHAPTER 10

SOLUTIONS FOR A HAPPIER PLANET

Congratulations! You've managed to get to the airport, get past security, board, take-off, and land without incident (even if you are humming tunes on a deserted island). Hooray! You are a survivor. Now, let's hope the airline industry can survive.

Flying passengers around the world in big planes is a tough business. Competition is fierce, fuel prices fluctuate wildly, and economic busts can wreak havoc on even the best-run airlines. Next are a few suggestions and cost-saving initiatives for airlines that might be struggling due to tough times. CEOs are welcome to contact me for detailed business plans. (If your annual report indicates any of these really did save your airline from bankruptcy, I should think a free round trip ticket for me and the companion of my choice might be a nice thank-you gift.)

BABIES IN THE BACK

If you don't have one of your own, chances are you don't like them, and you are especially not fond of sitting near them. Designate rows for crying babies in the rear of the plane. Charge an extra $5 per ticket for seats as far away from the baby section as possible. On an average-size plane, that could bring in an extra $1,500 in revenue per flight. Who wouldn't pay $5 for guaranteed peace and quiet? That's less than the cost of a cup of coffee.[41] (Such a brilliant and obvious solution, I can't understand why it hasn't been thought of before.)

ORGANIZE ROWS BY DRINK PREFERENCES

Everyone who wants orange juice, rows 1–10. Soda, rows 11–20. Alcoholic beverages, to the rear of the plane, where the party never ends. (I'm already putting the crying babies back there anyway, so might as well crack out the tequila and start crying in your beers—if you can't beat 'em, join 'em.) Seating by drink preference will eliminate having to take drink orders, for a cost savings of one flight attendant per flight. If you can get everyone on the plane to just agree to drink Sierra Mist and buy two-liter bottles in bulk instead of individual cans, even better.

DESIGNATE ONE AIRPLANE PER FLEET AS THE "VACATION PLANE"

Remember the movies in the '70s when tourists would step out of a plane in Hawaii and women in hula skirts would hang a lei around their necks? Now that's customer service. It's just common sense to understand that passengers will start spending their money as soon as they feel they are on vacation. For flights heading to a golf destination, remove the first ten rows to create a makeshift putting green, and add a few extra dollars to the price of tickets. For planes heading to Vegas,

---

41. Well, it's less than a venti double-mocha frappuccino with an extra shot of espresso, plus tax.

install a few slot machines in the galley, a bar in the middle of the plane, and swap out the male flight attendants for Chippendales dancers. Does your airline offer service to The Bahamas? If so, offer rows that come with a sunroof so passengers can avoid showing up at the beach as white as a ghost. Imagine the tan you can get that close to the sun. (Passengers might lose a year or two from their life with a little melanoma, but really, you can't put a price on looking good.)

BOOZE CRUISE AT THIRTY THOUSAND FEET

You've seen one in every major city located near water. The giant party boat goes out thirty feet from the shore and all hell breaks loose. What about the poor inland cities in the Midwest, starving for a little spring break–style action? Let's get some of the unused planes off the runway and up in the air and let these folks have a good time. $99 gets you an open bar, an '80s cover band, go-go dancers—the works. Best time you can possibly have in a holding pattern.

START A REALITY TV SHOW

If you own a plane you have what TV executives want: a captive audience of strangers dying for their fifteen minutes of fame. Install hidden cameras in the seatbacks and start filming everyone *Taxi Cab Confession*–style. Hire professional actors for flight attendants to ask the passengers provoking questions. "Good morning Mr. Johnson. Would you care for coffee or tea? How about you Mrs. Johnson? Oh, and Mrs. Johnson, did you happen to notice Mr. Johnson has lowered his armrest and his hand is resting very close to the thigh of the woman sleeping next to him? How do you feel about that? Oh, and if you could lean forward when you speak please that would be great . . ."

OTHER COST-SAVING/INDUSTRY-SAVING INITIATIVES

- Pay cash instead of credit at the pump when filling up the planes.

- Install a karaoke machine on board. They always save a failing business.

- Charge $25 to let people drive the plane for a while. Charge $50 if they want to attempt a landing.

- Designate one bathroom "#2 free," and charge a buck or two to use it. May be tough to monitor if anyone abuses the rule, so you'll have to go by the honor system.

- Try again to get everyone on the plane to drink Sierra Mist so you can buy two-liter bottles. Or maybe you should consider installing a soda fountain. I'm convinced those individual cans of beverages are more expensive than you think. At least that's what I assume, since I've always been met with a disapproving frown anytime I've asked for the whole can of soda. It's not my fault I'm thirsty. You made me eat the pretzels.

Additional note to airline CEOs: The bottom line is, whatever you ultimately decide to do to save the airlines, please stop charging us for our bags. It's not our fault we need to carry everything we own with us. If we leave our stuff at home our relatives will put it on eBay. Times are tough.

CHAPTER 11

PLEASE HUG ME AWARDS

The World's Craziest Stories About Flying Machines and Blue Poop

Just for fun, compiled here are the winners of the *Please Hug Me* Awards for the craziest stories from the past few decades of air travel. Each one guaranteed to bore your spouse, amuse your friends, and kill a little more time at the airport, on your flight, or in your new island home. Yup, they're all true.

MOST UNUSUAL LANDING

In 2008, August Gorreck (now that's a name) casually landed a 1930s biplane on top of a tree in East Windsor, Connecticut. The antique plane lost power just after taking off, and Gorreck glided it down to rest on the top of a group of trees, about fifty feet in the air, and waited until the fire department came to rescue him. No one was injured, except for possibly a small, rather shocked squirrel.

WORST CASE OF PREMATURE FIRING

This award works on so many levels. On March 22, 2008, Captain James Langenhahn was stowing his holstered pistol in preparation for landing a US Airways flight in Charlotte, North Carolina, when the gun went off. The shot exited the left side of the plane and did little damage, but the airline fired the veteran pilot immediately. Unfortunately, they had no idea what a backlash of bad press this would cause. It seems Langenhahn was not the first to complain about the questionable new rule requiring a TSA-mandated padlock be placed through a hole in the holster, right against the trigger of a loaded gun. Okay, now let those premature firing jokes run wild.

BEST STORY ABOUT ALMOST GETTING HIT IN THE HEAD WITH HUMAN WASTE

In 2003, Ray Erickson of Santa Cruz, California, won $3,236 in a lawsuit against American Airlines when two pieces of blue ice came crashing through the skylights of his boat. He tracked the two chunks of frozen toilet waste, commonly referred to as blue ice, to American Airlines Flight 1950. Erickson claimed a leak caused the waste to build up on the outside of the aircraft, where it eventually dropped off like an icicle.

A month later the ruling was overturned when it was determined Flight 1950 was on the ground at the time the poop crashed down on the boat. Unfortunately, no other airline has rushed forward to claim responsibility for the falling doodoo, leaving Erickson out a couple of expensive skylights. Of course, no one thought to ask if perhaps the blue ice simply came from the digestive system of a very large and very cold bird.

MOST EMBARRASSING AIRCRAFT MOVEMENT

In 2001, reports of a female passenger becoming vacuum sealed to an airline toilet circled the globe with lightning speed (as only stories of

this nature can). As the legend goes, the rather large woman was flying across the Atlantic on a Scandinavia Airlines Boeing 767 when
she found herself stuck to the seat after she flushed, and was forced to
remain on the throne for the duration of the flight. Mechanics were
finally able to pry her loose after the aircraft landed. (It's unclear if the
mechanics also had to wipe.)

Several weeks following the report the airline retracted the story,
claiming it a hoax. The ordeal spawned numerous debates on websites
and chat boards such as poopreport.com (cleverly designed in brown,
complete with brown fonts), along with a string of cheesy one-liners
like, "She was flushed with anger." The story has also become a textbook entry for learning verbs in an English as Second Language course
(I sh-t you not), and it even warranted a MythBuster episode on Dis-
covery Channel, to determine if it was actually possible to vacuum seal
oneself to a toilet.

My theory? You simply can't make this kind of stuff up. And people really need to get a life.

WORST JOB AT GIVING CREDIT WHERE CREDIT IS DUE

Langley Air Force Base in Virginia and NASA's Langley Research
Center are named after Samuel Pierpont Langley, credited by the
Smithsonian with inventing the first flying machine, even though his
invention fell like a sack of bricks into the Potomac River. Number of
airports or historic buildings named after Wilbur and Orville Wright,
the true pioneers of modern flight? One half.

The brothers share Wright-Patterson Air Force Base in Dayton,
Ohio (which allegedly housed the famed wreckage from the UFO
crash in Roswell, New Mexico, in 1947), with fallen U.S. Army pilot,
Frank Stuart Patterson. But, the brothers' legacy lives on in full at The

Wright Brothers Steak House in Burlington, North Carolina, named solely in their honor.

BEST JOB AT BALANCING THE BUDGET

In 1987, American Airlines saved $40,000 by eliminating one olive from each salad served in first class. It is undetermined how many olive farmers lost their jobs as a result. Not to be outdone, Southwest Airlines followed suit, and in 2000 removed three peanuts from each bag for a savings of $300,000.

COOLEST UNDER PRESSURE

If you happen to be on a plane and the engine falls off, you're gonna want to be seated next to this anonymous passenger. On a flight departing from Cape Town, South Africa, in November 2007, a loud bang ten minutes into the flight worked passengers into a frenzy. When the distraught passengers began shouting and screaming, "What was that?!" the man with the clearest view out the window calmly replied, "That's our engine that's just fallen off." He then explained that a plane can very easily fly on one engine, and presumably went back to completing his Sudoku. As predicted, the plane jettisoned some fuel then made a smooth landing.

MOST CONFUSING HISTORY OF A BAND NAME WITH THE WORD *AIRPLANE* IN IT

Jefferson Airplane, the great psychedelic band of the '60s and '70s, wins this award hands down. The group was responsible for a string of Top

20 albums (and a whole lot of kids doing a whole lot of drugs) before they eventually evolved into the band known as Jefferson Starship, then Starship Jefferson, and finally Starship.

In 1988, singer Grace Slick reformed the original Jefferson Airplane, which released one further album before being inducted into the Rock and Roll Hall of Fame in 1996, while Starship went on to become Paul Kantner's Wooden Ships, which in turn then became Jefferson Starship: The Next Generation, before finally returning to Jefferson Starship. (None of this is a joke.)

CITY WITH THE WORST AIRPORT CODE

Sioux City, Iowa. Their airport code? SUX. The unfortunate city made several attempts to have its three-letter designator code changed, only to have the FAA offer five equally embarrassing alternatives, including GAY (which they have apparently been saving until a new colony breaks off from San Francisco). In true American spirit, Sioux City has turned their misfortunate into profit, selling T-shirts, caps, and bumper stickers that read Fly SUX, Work SUX, etc.

CITY WITH THE SECOND WORSE AIRPORT CODE

Fukuoka, Japan, with the airport code FUK. (Or it could be the best, depending on how you look at it)

Hug Me Bonus: More Fun Facts (Free of Charge)

- Commercial airplanes range from $50 million for a basic 737, to $300 million for a brand-new top-of-the-line 747. Add another $50 if you want the 5-disc CD changer.

- In 1997 Boeing merged with McDonnell Douglas to become the largest manufacturer of commercial aircraft in the world. They also operate the Space Shuttle and the International Space Station, with plans to open a fast-food chain on the moon.

- All of the passengers, flight crew, and luggage combined account for less than 10 percent of a plane's bulk weight. The majority is jet fuel.

- Most airplanes average a little less than half a mile to the gallon. That works out to about seven thousand gallons of fuel needed for a cross-country flight. Now you understand exactly why the price of oil is so important.

- In all my years of being single, I never once sat next to an attractive female on a flight. The moment I find myself in a relationship, I'm seated next to lonely swimsuit models and entire female volleyball teams, all complaining they need backrubs.

- Due to pressurization, it is impossible to open the airplane doors while airborne. So don't worry about the guy who appears suicidal sitting next to you. He's not going anywhere.

- Raising the window shades for landing has nothing to do with letting more light in the plane or flight attendants with OCD. They are required to be up in order for passengers to remain oriented if there is an accident.

- Pilots typically are not allowed to have beards. This has little to do with personal hygiene or the fact that beards look ridiculous on anyone except professional hockey players. A beard could stop the oxygen mask from fitting tightly enough if the cabin pressure dropped suddenly.

- The first women flight attendants in 1930 were required to weigh no more than 115 pounds, be nurses, and unmarried. Can you spell *sexy*? (Just kidding . . .)

- Generally, lower flight numbers are assigned to more prestigious routes. For example, flight number one might be reserved for New York to Paris, D.C. to London, or Los Angeles to the Betty Ford Rehab Clinic.

- The average number of people airborne over the United States at any given hour is sixty-one thousand. (Does not include people in hot air balloons and kids climbing trees.)

- The abbreviation ORD for Chicago's O'Hare Airport comes from the old name 'Orchard Field.'

- If you are taking off from runway 90, it doesn't mean there are eighty-nine other runways at your airport. Runway numbers correspond with magnetic points of the compass and are often referred to by their degree designation, with the most common being 09, 18, 27, 36 for 90, 180, 270, and 360 degrees respectively.

- When boredom strikes, you can track the progress of any flight on a variety of websites, including FlightAware.com, Flightview.com, FlyteComm.com, Fboweb.com, or by using Google Earth. You can also try to run really fast on the ground and see how long you can follow the plane.

- Hijacking of airplanes was outlawed in 1961.

- No U.S. airline currently travels to Africa.

CHAPTER 12

QUIZ TIME!

Well, as with any good textbook, I would be remiss if I allowed you to exit the plane and proceed to baggage claim without one final quiz. It's my sincere hope that you've enjoyed this book, and that it has served its purpose, namely, to put a smile on your face or a chuckle in your heart while sitting through a long flight or unexpected delay. And don't forget—no matter where your journeys may take you, be sure to treat everyone you meet with courtesy and respect, and smile whenever you can. Cussing will not get you home any faster. Besides, nobody likes a meanie.

Remember, a flight is like a Broadway show you paid hundreds of dollars for tickets to see, where the performers are scared to death of losing their job. Applaud those who do good work. Cheer wildly for great landings and excellent service. And try to keep the aisles clear at all times. And yes, if your pilot bumps into a mountain, you are entitled to boo. Just don't throw peanuts at him. That will send the message that we don't appreciate those honey-roasted bags of salted ecstasy, after we worked so hard to get them back. (Throw the pretzels.)

In the meantime, keep your head up and follow the rules you've learned here, and you just may find these not-so-friendly skies turning cheery and blue for you once again. And if you're a parent with a couple of kids, do them a favor and take them to Disney World. Hmm … come to think of it, maybe that's where I'll take my parents. It's been a long time coming.

I do hope you enjoyed your flight. And sorry again if you were delayed, but you know, had you not been, perhaps we might never have met.

TEST YOUR KNOWLEDGE TRIVIA

Feel free to write down your score and ask your flight attendant if you can turn your points in for frequent flyer miles. You can't, but it will be a nice icebreaker to use if you'd like to ask them for their number. (My final gift to you.)

1. What is the world's largest airline?

2. What is the world's busiest airport?

3. Where is the world's biggest airport terminal?

4. What is the oldest airline in the world?

5. Who was the first U.S. president to ride in an airplane?

6. What popular car manufacturer makes airplane engines for Boeing?

7. What professional basketball player starred in the 1980 comedy, *Airplane!* in the role of Roger Murdock?

8. Who wrote the song "Jet Airliner"?

9. In the famous final scene of *Casablanca*, where is the plane carrying Victor Laszlo (Paul Henreid) and Ilsa Lund (Ingrid Bergman) headed?

10. What was the name of the airline that had the big bang sound from the left wing that caused my fear of flying?

Answers:

1. *American Airlines. The combined fleet is the largest in the world, with more than a thousand aircraft, operating more than four thousand flights daily in more than 40 countries.*

2. *Hartsfield-Jackson Atlanta International Airport, Atlanta, Georgia, which handles both the largest number of passengers, most arrivals and departures, and most destinations. Chicago's O'Hare International Airport held this title with an airplane taking off or landing every thirty-seven seconds, up until 1999 (suspiciously, the same year Michael Jordan retired).*

3. *Beijing Capital International Airport's Terminal 3. From end to end the dragon-like design is two miles in length. All five of Heathrow International's terminals could fit inside.*

4. *KLM Royal Dutch Airlines, based in Amstelveen, Netherlands, and founded in 1919. (In the United States, both Northwest Airlines and United Airlines claim to be the oldest, each founded in 1926.)*

5. *Franklin Delano Roosevelt*

6. *Rolls Royce*

7. *Kareem Abdul-Jabbar*

8. *"Jet Airliner," the Steve Miller Band hit, was actually written by the late, blind singer-songwriter Paul Pena for his second album* New Train, *recorded in 1973. Steve Miller heard a copy of "Jet Airliner" and decided to record it with his own band, where it reached number 8 on the charts. Due to a contract dispute, Pena's album wasn't released until 2000, twenty-seven years after it was recorded, and just a few years before his death in 2005.*

9. *Lisbon*

10. *Air Italia (I told you there'd be a quiz later.)*

HOME AT LAST

The Miracle of US Air Flight 1549

Before the chapter about conquering your fear of flying, I asked you to read a little passage reminding you that you never have to hear or read another news story about a plane that had trouble taking off or landing, and that you were going to land perfectly safely. (And how was your landing by the way?) I'm guessing you went along with it, probably because you had little else to do at the time. And now that you're here at the end of the book, I'm guessing you want to know what exactly I was getting at, and if I lost my mind. Fair enough.

Whenever I used to hear or read a news story about a plane crash, it struck me in a very personal manner, as I think it does a great many people. Because we all have that fear that it could have just as easily been us, or worse, we might've been forced to make that call to the airlines to see if our loved ones were on the list of people who boarded that plane. It's a terrible feeling. While I have been fortunate to never know anyone who has died in a plane crash, I had a very dear friend killed in a car accident, so I understand what it's like to have someone ripped from your life in such a violent, unexpected manner. It's been years and I still miss him every day.

If you've lost someone close to you, or harbor the fear that you might, perhaps you feel that sometimes these things are beyond our control. Accidents can happen. But living in fear of an accident happening is well within our control. And when you learn to control your fears, you will very often find those events you used to worry about simply vanish from your existence. Magic? Not exactly.

As I mentioned before, I had a fear of flying for a great many years. For years I was envious of the people who could go to sleep on a plane and not worry that anything catastrophic was going to happen. That voice in the back of my mind was always there. You know the voice, so I don't have to tell you.

Then, one day I discovered something, and the voice vanished.

I discovered that we can truly control our own destiny. We have a choice in deciding what events we wish to bring into our lives, and which events we don't. We can choose to lead happy, fulfilled lives full of love and laughter, or we can choose to live in fear of things. And when we choose to live in fear of things, very often these fears come true.

I'm sure you know people who worry incessantly about losing their job, and guess what? They're the first to get laid off when the economy tanks. Or they're so worried about their partner cheating on them that guess what? They find out they've been cheated on. Point is, when you constantly worry about something, even a random event like being audited, being in a car accident, or being a victim of a robbery, you are opening yourself up for these events to occur in your life. Why? Because by dwelling on these very things you don't want, you have given power to these thoughts. And when thoughts are given power, they very often find a way to become real. Just as every single thing in your life was at one point nothing more than a mere thought.

So, if you never think about your airplane having trouble with taking off or landing, will you enjoy smooth flying forever? Most would say, no, it makes no difference.

I say this is where it gets interesting.

I want to leave you with one last story, one that I'm sure you recall. It's the story of US Air Flight 1549 that departed from LaGuardia airport in New York on January 15, 2009, and minutes into the flight encountered a flock of birds that got caught up in the engines, rendering not one, but both engines useless. The plane had yet to reach an altitude high enough where the pilot could turn around and make an emergency landing on a runway. Instead, his only choice was to land the plane in the middle of the Hudson River.

Big, lumbering, commercial jets aren't particularly designed to land in rivers. In fact, most comedians like to make fun of the safety announcements about water landings being entirely pointless. Never before Flight 1549 has an airplane landed in the water and not suffered some kind of catastrophic damage. Do you know why Flight 1549 landed safely in the Hudson and all 155 passengers and crew on board exited the plane and simply stood on the wings and waited while the ferries chugged up to pull them out of the water? Because the pilot, Captain Chesley Sullenberger, believed he was going to land the plane in the Hudson, and all 155 people were going to simply walk off. He believed he could do the impossible. Fear never entered his mind. And that kind of revolutionary thinking is happening all around the world right now. I want you to keep that thought in your mind while we finish up here—because here comes the fun part.

Earlier, I asked you to believe for a moment as I believe, which is every plane will take off and land exactly as it's intended. Now, hopefully you've enjoyed this book enough to recommend it to a friend, and hopefully your friend enjoys it enough to do the same thing. Of course they have more friends than you, so they can recommend it to several more people. And now we're all thinking and more important, BELIEVING the same thing, which is *every plane will take off and land exactly as it's intended.*

Each of our individual thoughts creates a ripple effect that affects all the other thoughts in the world. The stronger our thoughts, and the more people thinking those same thoughts, the stronger the ripple we cause. If the entire world purged its collective fear of flying from its mind, I believe we would greatly reduce the risk of accidents involving airplanes. Because without fear, there would be no power to attract the reality of that fear into our world. In essence, a global awakening.

Now, I have no doubt you are a highly intelligent person, and you're immediately thinking, well, sure. We can all go ahead and believe things will be fine, but sometimes accidents happen anyway. Or, you may say, well, how would that take into account all of the past stories of airplane tragedies, and an event like 9/11? Certainly the people on those flights weren't all afraid of flying and that's why something bad happened.

No, certainly not. But just because something happened in the past, does not mean it needs to happen again. We don't need events we can't control in our world. And if we learn to take control of our fears, we are taking the first step to reaching this goal.

Can the collective thoughts of a great number of individuals affect the destiny of others? Yes, I believe they can. Look at those who have cured their terminal cancer with the help of prayer groups. Or those who have achieved the seemingly impossible, like leading an entire country from times of war to times of peace and prosperity because they've had the thoughts and beliefs of millions of individuals aiding them.

Couldn't a raised consciousness help those in charge of a plane's maintenance and safe operation maintain a greater focus on their job? Couldn't a greater awareness put those in charge more in tune with "hunches" or instincts that we all feel from time to time, perhaps recognizing and preventing a dangerous situation before it occurs? There are a great many forces at work in our universe, and we're all a lot more connected than we'd like to think.

And a collective thought has to start somewhere. In this case, it starts with you.

This is a big concept, and certainly one that warrants much more than a little note at the end here, but my job is just to plant the seed. I would encourage you to do a little exploring on your own, and for a broader discussion of this topic, please visit us at www.pleasehugme series.com. Thoughts have an energy all their own that operate on a quantum level we are just beginning to understand. There are some wonderful books out there discussing this principle. The idea that we can control every aspect of our lives is still pretty new to us, but within the next century, we're going to see some amazing changes taking place. We really can control our own destinies, and it is my firm belief that eventually, this will lead to a new world where just by focusing on our intentions, even seemingly random events like accidents will begin to disappear, as we realize they are really not random at all.

Granted, that might sound a little far fetched. Crazy—the idea that just by removing our fear of events they will not be able to manifest themselves in our lives. Possibly. But if you lived one hundred years ago, and someone told you there would one day be an invention where you could go up in the sky and fly across the entire country in a matter of hours, you would've likely thought the same thing. Crazy is just a word for that which we can't understand.

You might also be wondering why I chose to include such a topic here, after all, this is supposed to be a humor book. But I think this is the best place to include it. Because you can't laugh and feel good about something and be afraid of something at the same time–those two feelings simply cannot exist simultaneously. If everyone is feeling good and laughing about flying, the fear of flying is gone. And maybe, just maybe, without that fear in the world, all we would ever know is safe flying. Isn't that worth a shot?

Because the invention of the airplane was designed to bring people together, not to tear us apart. And because we like stories like US Air Flight 1549. We really, really do.

AUTHOR'S NOTE

Just one more thing I want to mention. Since I began writing this, I haven't heard or read a story about a flight that didn't take off and land safely. Including the following:

- January 2008, British Airways Flight BA38 lost all power and the pilot had to glide the plane in, landed safely in the grass before reaching the runway.

- March 2008, Lufthansa Flight LH44 the left wing struck the ground as the plane was blown across the runway after being caught in a crosswind. The pilot landed the plane safely on the second attempt.

- May 2008, Dallas, Texas, a pilot landed a private plane safely *on top of another plane* attempting to take off on same runway.

- July 2008, a Midwest Airlines pilot lost control of the up-and-down movement of the aircraft he was piloting after an emergency evacuation slide inflated inside the tail. (Worthy of noting, the plane was carrying then presidential candidate, Senator Obama.)

- July 2008, Qantas Flight 30 the cargo door blew off and ripped an enormous hole in the fuselage while at thirty thousand feet. The pilot landed the plane safely.

- September 2008, after losing power, a 1930s biplane landed safely *in a tree* in East Windsor, Connecticut.

- January 2009, US Air Flight 1549 lost both engines after encountering a flock of birds. The pilot landed the plane safely in the Hudson River.

- April 2009, in Tampa, Florida, a passenger landed a private plane safely after the pilot died during the flight.

Look them all up. That's hundreds of people who walked away from planes that had some sort of problem in the past year who very well might not have walked away. Could've been just luck. Could've been that people are tired of hearing about stories with unhappy endings and are demanding something else. Either way, it can't hurt to focus your thoughts on the continued safe landings of airplanes every chance that you can!

TEAR-OUT FORMS FOR SURVIVING OVERNIGHT AIRPORT DELAYS

INSTRUCTIONS: Tear out page and place on chest while sleeping on airport chair.

- - ✂ - ✂

PLEASE DO NOT CALL SECURITY.

I'M NOT HOMELESS. I'VE BEEN DELAYED.

PLEASE WAKE ME AT _____ AM/PM FOR MY FLIGHT.

ALSO, PLEASE DON'T STEAL MY WALLET.

MANY THANKS!

☺

- - ✂ - ✂

NO LLAME POR FAVOR LA SEGURIDAD.

NO SOY SIN HOGAR. ME HAN RETRASADO.

DESPIÉRTEME POR FAVOR EN EL _____ AM/PM PARA
MI VUELO. TAMBIÉN, NO ROBE POR FAVOR MI
CARPETA.

¡MUCHAS GRACIAS!

:~)

✂ -

BITTE BENENNEN SIE NICHT SICHERHEIT.

ICH BIN NICHT HEIMATLOS. ICH BIN VERZÖGERT WORDEN.

WECKEN SIE MICH BITTE AM _____ AM/PM FÜR MEINEN

FLUG AUF. AUCH BITTE STEHLEN SIE

NICHT MEINE MAPPE.

VIEL DANK!

:+)

✂ -

不要叫治安 我不是无家可归的 我被延迟了

请叫醒我在我_____ AM/PM 的航班出发时间。并且，

不要窃取我的钱包。

非常感谢

^_^

COMPANIES THAT NOW OWE ME A FREE T-SHIRT

FOR MENTIONING SOMETHING NICE ABOUT THEM

(Men's medium)

Airfarewatchdog.com
Airportbooties.com
American Express
Bing.com
Consumerwebwatch.com
EarPlanes
Famousmormons.net
FlightStats.com
Jaunted.com
Luggageforward.com
Luggagefree.com
Magellans.com
SeatGuru.com
Sidestep.com
Southwest Airlines
Sportsexpress.com
Theluggageclub.com
Turbulenceforecast.com
Virgin Airlines

Websites You'll Want To Remember

Don't forget to check out these great sites...

SmellNoEvil.net. Protect those feet going through security with Airport Booties™.

FearofFlying.com. Cure that fear already!

Points.com. Track your frequent flyer miles and swap your points with other point-swappers.

Zenclasstravel.com. Never misplace any of your belongings again with the Nirvana Seatback Organizer.

And be sure to visit **Pleasehugmeseries.com** for even more travel products, special offers, additional Airport Time Wasters, and other Please Hug Me titles.

CELEBRITIES MENTIONED IN THIS BOOK

RANKED BY COOLNESS FACTOR

(Who should also send me a free T-shirt)

Al Pacino
Tiger Woods
Bruce Springsteen
George Clooney
Billy Joel
Conan O'Brien
Jack Cousteau
Bill Cosby
Dennis Miller
Bob Costas
Pamela Anderson
Claudia Schiffer
Giada
Julia Roberts
Ray Romano
Chevy Chase
Pat Sajak

Tony Danza

Oprah

Lenny Kravitz

Tom Cruise

Al Gore

The Loch Ness Monster

La Toya Jackson

Mary-Kate and Ashley Olsen

David Hasselhoff

Keanu Reeves

Rick Astley

Carrot Top

James Blunt

Kevin Federline

ABOUT THE AUTHOR

Jeff Michaels is a humor writer and the author of two novels. He is also the founder and lead singer of Even Elroy (www.evenelroy.com), whose music can be heard on over 200 independent radio stations nationwide, and has been featured on *The Real World* (MTV), and in shows on USA Network, Oxygen, Lifetime, and in several independent films.

A hectic travel and performance schedule leaves him delayed more often than not, and he believes drastic measures are needed to help the one person forgotten amongst all the airline industry woes: the weary traveler. Hence, *Please Hug Me—I've Been Delayed* was born.

Michaels also claims to be a level-ten Sudoku player, even though he's been repeatedly told no such ranking exists.